DAY AFTER THE WASTE LAND

(A reimagining of T.S. Eliot's The Waste Land)

Words by Will Averill
Artwork by Kent Smith

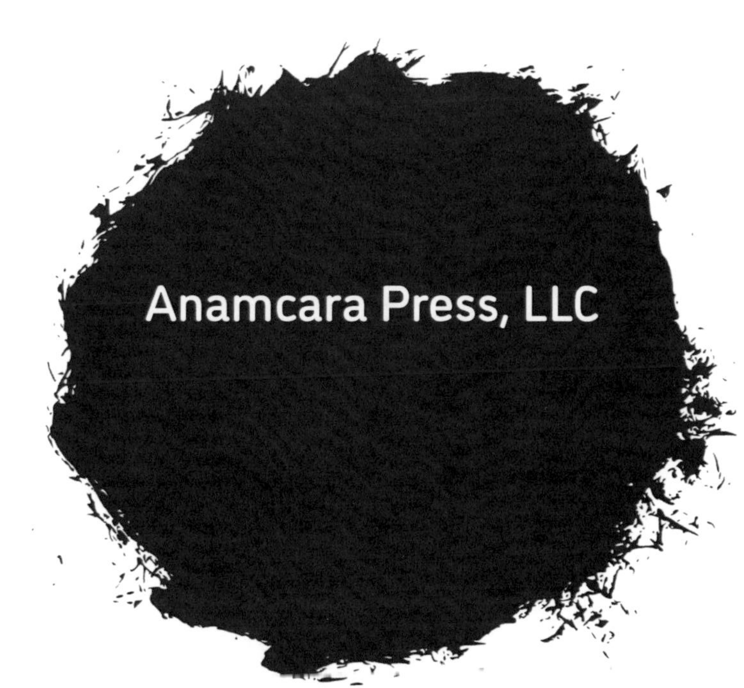

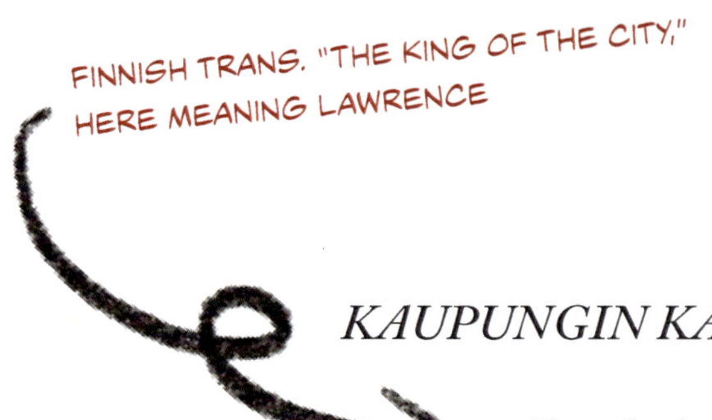

KAUPUNGIN KANSAN HERRA

For Andy Morton

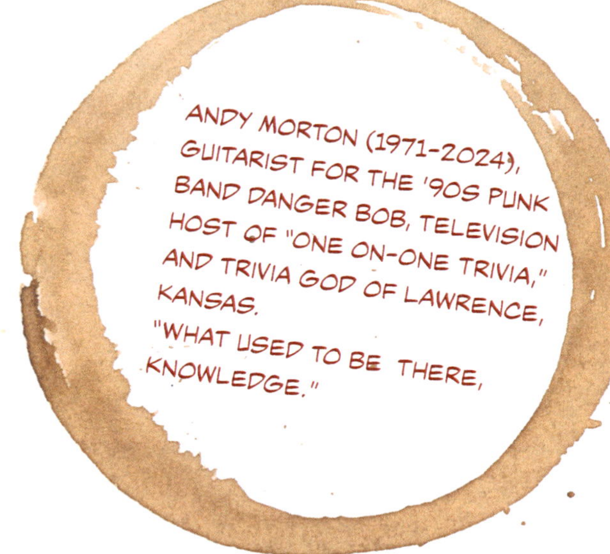

Published in 2025 by Anamcara Press LLC
Author © 2025 Will Averill
Artwork © 2025 Kent Smith
Book design by Amber Fraley
Fonts: *Might Makes Right BB, Houschka Rounded, DINosaur and Minion Pro.*
Printed in the United States of America.

Book Description: *Poetry meets pop culture and a small Midwest town becomes the "Unreal City" in Will Averill's "Day After the Waste Land," a reimagining of T.S. Eliot's classic poem through the streets, stories, and spirit of Lawrence, Kansas.*

ANAMCARA PRESS LLC
P.O. Box 442072, Lawrence, KS 66044
https://anamcara-press.com/

Quantity sales. For details, contact the publisher at the address above. Orders by U.S. trade bookstores and wholesalers. Please contact Ingram Distribution.

Averill, Will, Author
Smith, Kent, Artist
Day After The Waste Land

POE023040   POETRY / Subjects & Themes / Places
POE023000   POETRY / Subjects & Themes / General
ART023000 — ART / Popular Culture

ISBN-13: 978-1-960462-65-7 (Paperback)
ISBN-13: 978-1-960462-67-1 (EBook)
Library of Congress Control Number: 2025945679

Printed in the United States of America, KCMO

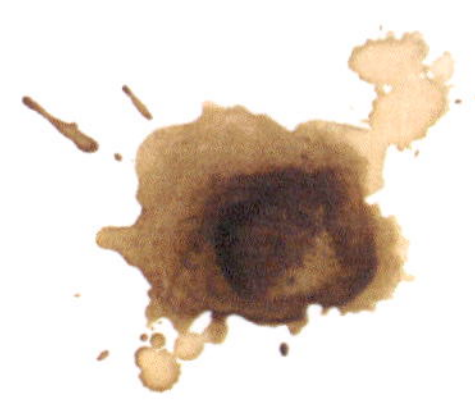

Contents

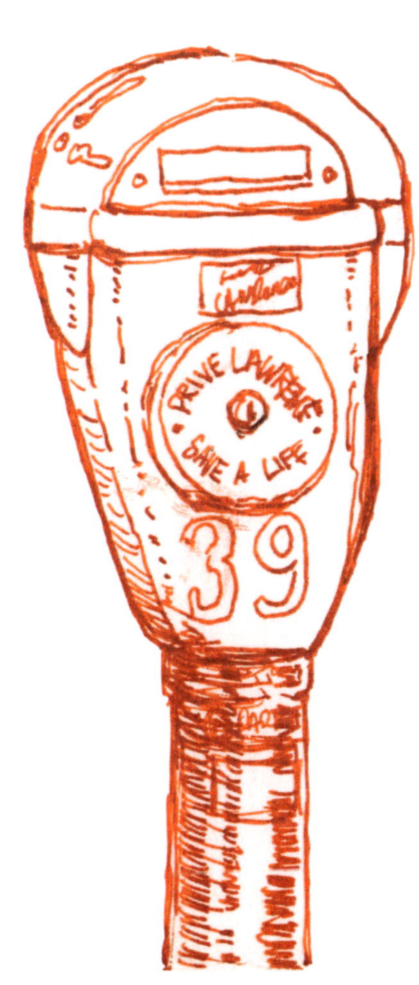

Roots
Western
R.C. DANIEL
SLAVE
JAZZ INCLUDES
John Colt
DAVE BRUBECK
HANK WILLIAMS
Owens
Dolly Parton
GOLTER
Towns Van Zandt
Don Cherri
Norma
CHET BAKER
Chris Stapleton
CHUCK MEAD
SHOVELS & ROPE
Joshua Abra
BIG BILL BRO AND PETE SEE GANG
mono
$7
JOHN ABERCROM SIGHE
FEATURING

INTRODUCTION

Day After The Waste Land: A Reimagining of T.S. Eliot's Masterpiece in the Context of My Hometown, Lawrence, Kansas.

"Still, she cried, and still the world pursues"

T.S. Eliot's *The Waste Land* has weaved through my life regularly and at some of my most pivotal moments, so this reimagining is a celebration of our continual collisions.

I first encountered *The Waste Land* in college—I wrote a full-length play called *Tales from the Waste Land* because I thought it sounded badass—part modernist, part dystopian, with a nod to The Who's *Baba O'Reily*, (a.k.a *Teenage Wasteland)*. The director of that play, Don Schawang, introduced me to Eliot's poem. One line in particular, "These fragments have a shored against my ruins," was used in his production notes, and so, in my very scattered late collegiate way, I skimmed through the poem, finding it dense and tiresome, and chucked it aside for a while. Still, I thought it was a cool title.

I moved to England in 2003, and in many ways, England is where my adulthood began. When you're out of your element, and your country, you grasp at familiarity, at camaraderie, through friends, books, and poems. In trying to find meaning in an ex-pat's life, I once again encountered Eliot—himself an American living and working in London, both subjects of *The Waste Land*. I went back to the poem, and this time, it resonated with me more—its emptiness, its uncertainty, the manic highs and lows—all felt true of a soul that was experiencing a great adventure, but also the loss of so much that had been familiar to me.

After that, a tradition formed organically: every few years, I would pick up *The Waste Land* and read it, seeing what I would find reflected in it in my life. I found a copy with annotations, which was hugely helpful, as so much of the poem is referential and modernist in name-checking and sampling from mythology and literature. This sampling, which to me seemed akin to hip-hop artists using samples of songs in beats, and which seemed so dense and inaccessible in my early reads, became one of the things I loved most about the work.

At its heart, this is what *The Waste Land* does so well—it's a beautiful piece in its own right. Eliot is a poetic mixmaster, pulling fragments from across Eastern and Western thought, poetry and literature, to create a mad verbal decoupage of loss and despair. It was a cacophony that shouldn't have worked but somehow did, like the sampling of Soul Coughing's Mark Degli Antoni, sending one's mind spinning, alternating between lyrical and brutal, with references like a hall of mirrors reflecting on themselves, spilling out at a breakneck pace, to be picked through by the reader.

Returning to my beloved hometown of Lawrence in 2012, I was struck by the need to process my eight-year absence. There is a natural dissociation that comes with leaving your home for so long. The changes in my hometown, though subtle, were significant in the context of my dual existence in England and Kansas. I embarked on a quest to merge my experiences in the United Kingdom with my life in Lawrence, Kansas. These fragments.

And again, I came back to *The Waste Land*.

London. Unreal City. Mystery, fog, hustle, bustle, a million stories all happening in a million lives at all times. Where you are both the center of your world and completely anonymous—but couldn't the same be said of Lawrence, my hometown? It, too, has the flowing banks of the Kaw—not as monumental a waterway as the Thames, but a source of power, an inexorable stamp of nature indelibly shaping the city's landscape.

Lawrence, like London, holds a cavalcade of identities—youth from the student population, education, and liberal arts through the university. Bedroom community commuters to state jobs in Topeka and tech gigs in Kansas City. A continually mid-20s service industry that spills into the bars at night and adds vibrancy, and underneath, out by the dam, the low thrum of thrown-up camps and shelters for the houseless.

Unreal. Lawrence is a Midwest city with a bloody past that has struggled between its desire for change and its firm Bible belt boundaries. "Lawrence is liberal, until you need it to be," the sheriff said to me, once, over beers at Louise's West.

Lawrence. Unreal City. I began to think it could work. This was in 2014 or so. I decided that I would take Eliot's poem, *The Waste Land*, and build it in Lawrence, Kansas. I would update the I would update the Modernist literary references so deftly weaved through Eliot's work through a modern pop culture lens of my Midwest hometown. I would work to create not just a parody poem, but a piece that could stand on its own merits as an exploration.

While movies get rebooted and bands cover songs, the reimagining of poetry is a less common endeavor. I found it challenging to explain my approach to this piece. After much contemplation, I settled on the term 'reimagining.' *Day After the Waste Land* is not a parody or an homage, though it contains elements of both. It is a radical rethinking, reshaping, and reexamining of the original text, infused with a modern pop culture lens.

Because *The Waste Land* is such a fantastic piece of work, the poem holds up well under the scrutiny of reimagination, and the work here, I believe, is a solid poem in its own right. I understand that I am settling comfortably on the shoulders of giants, and any beauty from this has been entirely in the quiet genius of the original work. I have mainly flitted here and there, coloring in the finer details, blotting out the fog with bright reds and blues, replacing chess boards with basketball hoops and updating the bars, words, jobs, and

places to modernize and reflect my beloved home.

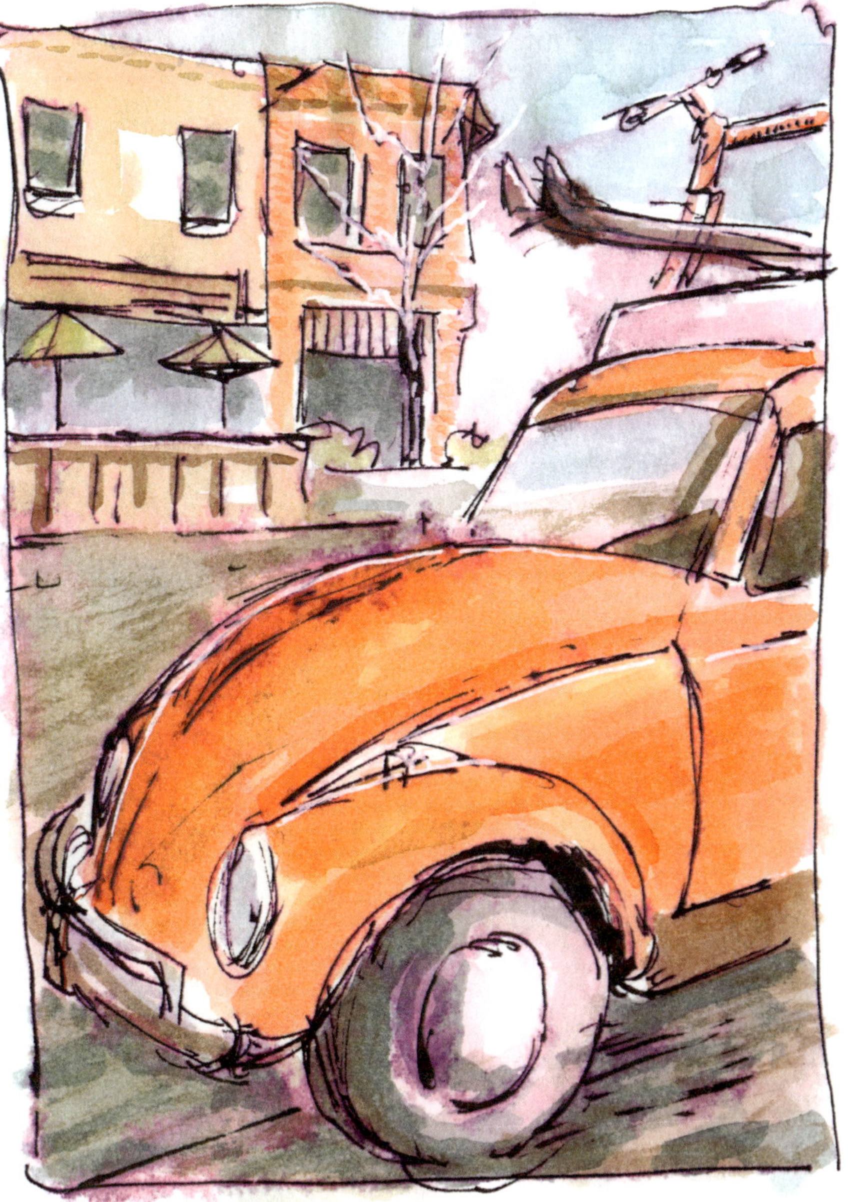

Realizing that the Venn diagram of people who love T.S. Eliot's *The Waste Land* and people who love Lawrence, Kansas was a small one, I took a page from Eliot's book and have added annotations to clarify some of the more mysterious stories and references for those readers who may not live in Lawrence or be familiar with its unique character. For instance, there was indeed a guy who used to keep his foot in a jar on his porch after having it cut off, and it is true that for a while, part of Einstein's brain was in a basement in Lawrence. These annotations serve to illuminate the unique character of my hometown, which is brimming with history in its own right, albeit a much more modern history than London's.

This poem was a collaborative effort, nurtured by the support of my amazing PBR Writer's Club—Chance Dibben, Maggie Bornholdt, Julia Gaughan, Aletha Schnake, Danny Caine, Rachel McCarthy-James, Richard Noggle and others who have contributed along the way. I am also deeply grateful for the unwavering support of my partner, friend, and love, Jacqueline Grunau, and my son Ollie. Thomas Fox Averill and Jeffrey Ann Goudie were both keen supporters and early readers of the idea, and I appreciated their familiarity both with Eliot and K.U. My folks, Ric and Jeanne Averill, who found their own indelible place in the flow of this town, and my sister Trish Neuteboom, her husband Eric, and Bella, Quincey, and Barrett, who in truth brought me back to Lawrence.

I would also like to express my gratitude to illustrator, artist, and friend Kent Smith for his invaluable input and work on the process—his sketches brought the essence of Lawrence to life with immediacy, power, and wry charm. Editor Amber Fraley took the chaotic blend of words and pictures and molded them into a unique book that celebrates its joyously unfinished nature. And big shout-outs to Micki from Anamcara Press for not flinching at the phrase "reimagined poetic classic."

Finally, Eliot dedicated his poem to his friend and mentor, Ezra Pound, and I felt my dedication should be equally meaningful. While I am a massive fan of LFK (Lawrence Fucking Kansas), my friend Andy Morton (1970-2024) will forever remain my go-to expert in what used to be where, which restaurants closed when, and general font of townie knowledge. The knowledge lost in his passing is irreplaceable, and to him, the King of Lawrence, I dedicate this meager and delightful creative endeavor.

—*Will Averill, June 28, 2025*

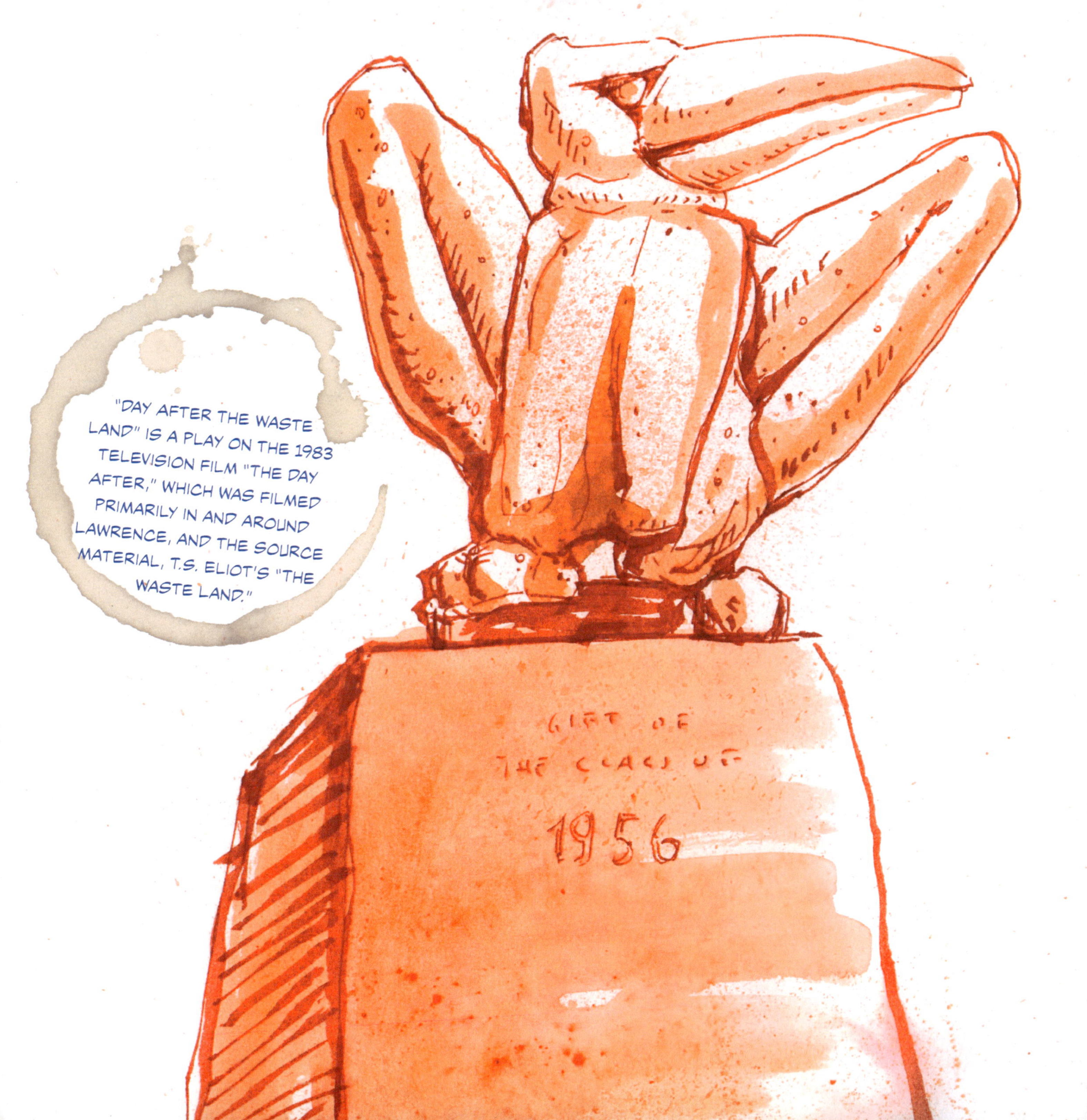
"DAY AFTER THE WASTE LAND" IS A PLAY ON THE 1983 TELEVISION FILM "THE DAY AFTER," WHICH WAS FILMED PRIMARILY IN AND AROUND LAWRENCE, AND THE SOURCE MATERIAL, T.S. ELIOT'S "THE WASTE LAND."
GIFT OF THE CLASS OF
1956

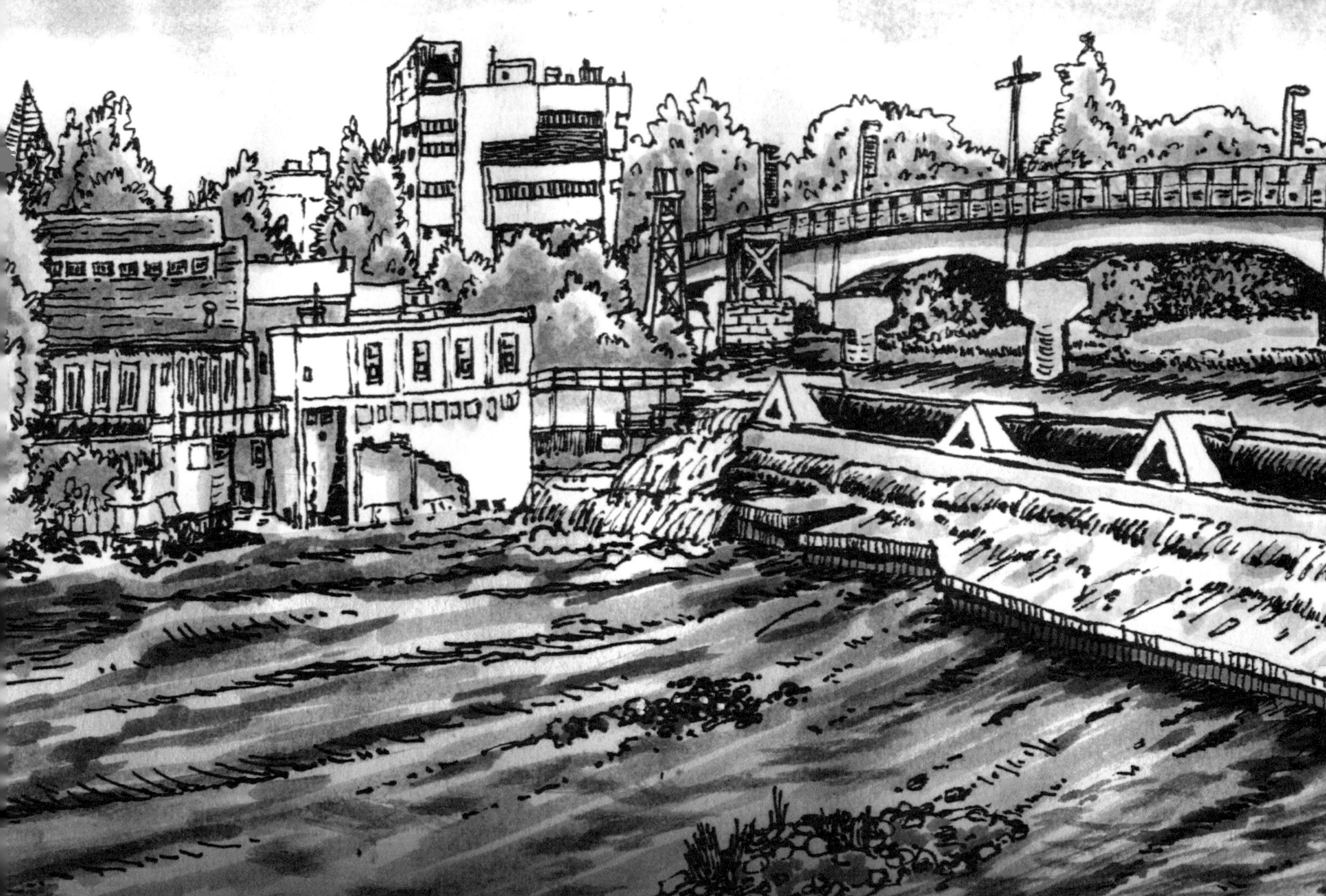

DAY AFTER THE
WASTE LAND
words by Will Averill
drawings by Kent Smith

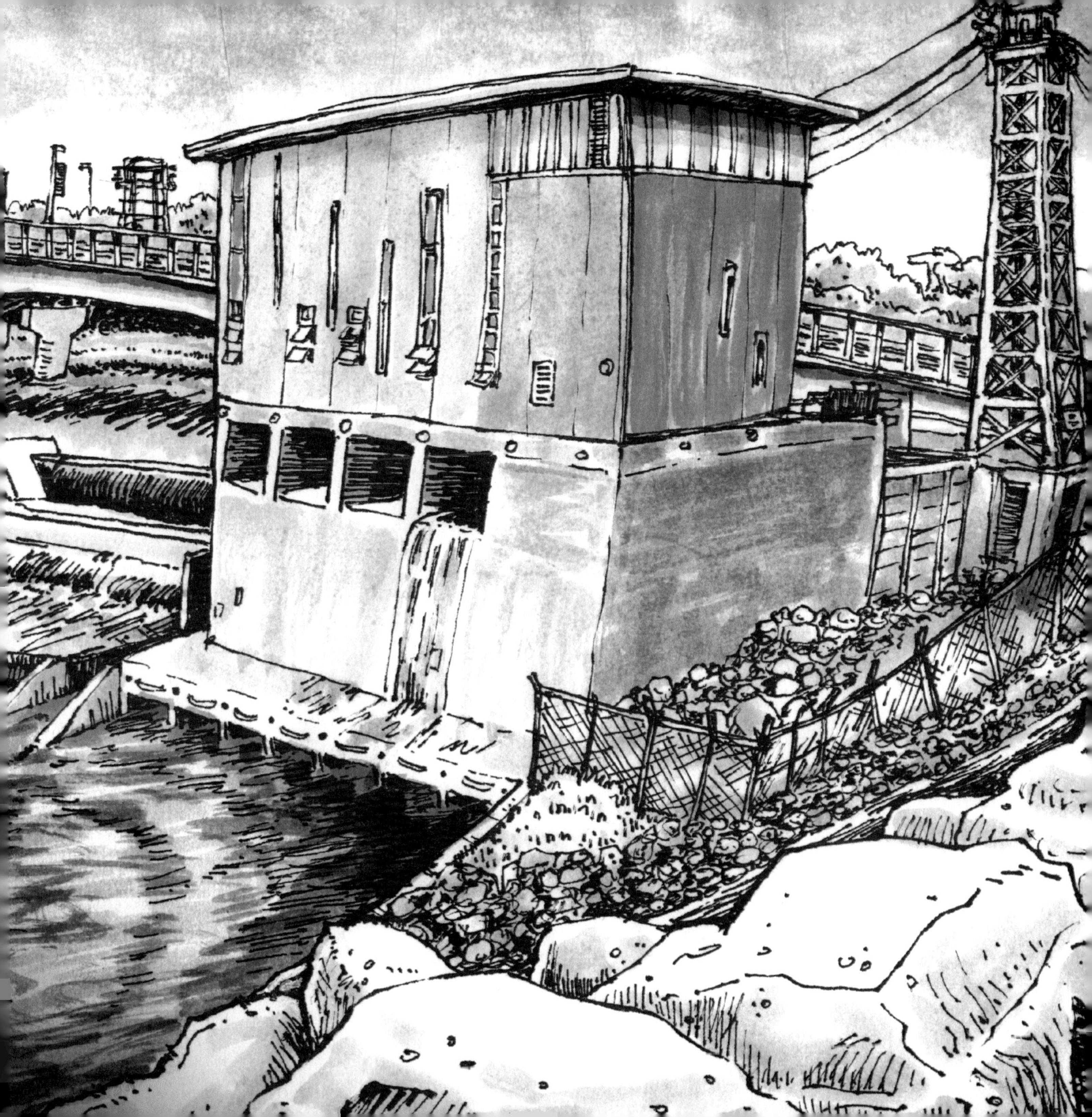

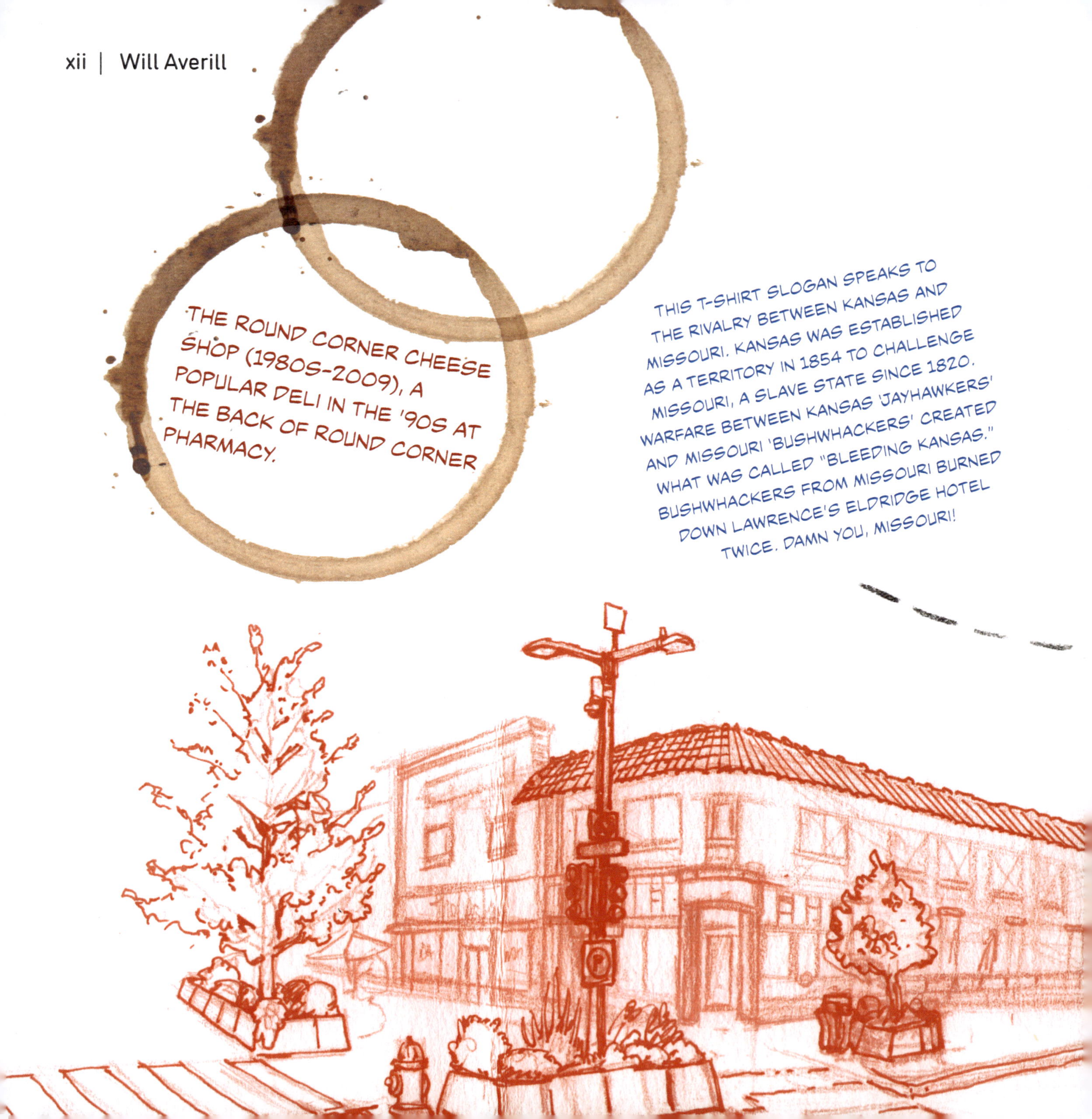

THE ROUND CORNER CHEESE SHOP (1980S-2009), A POPULAR DELI IN THE '90S AT THE BACK OF ROUND CORNER PHARMACY.

THIS T-SHIRT SLOGAN SPEAKS TO THE RIVALRY BETWEEN KANSAS AND MISSOURI. KANSAS WAS ESTABLISHED AS A TERRITORY IN 1854 TO CHALLENGE MISSOURI, A SLAVE STATE SINCE 1820. WARFARE BETWEEN KANSAS 'JAYHAWKERS' AND MISSOURI 'BUSHWHACKERS' CREATED WHAT WAS CALLED "BLEEDING KANSAS." BUSHWHACKERS FROM MISSOURI BURNED DOWN LAWRENCE'S ELDRIDGE HOTEL TWICE. DAMN YOU, MISSOURI!

I. Cheese Shoppe's Lament

March is the maddest month, breeding

frat boys from the Hill, mixing

basketball and desire, stirring

dull academics with tedious complaints.

Munchers kept us warm, covering

cream cheese with white frosting, feeding

a little life with day-old orange mini-cinnis.

Summer surprised us, coming over the Oread

with a gust of hot wind, we stopped on Eleventh,

Blown to Here, down the hill, into the stadium,

and tailgated, played cornhole for an hour.

Kansas: Keeping America Safe from Missouri since 1854.

And when we were children, staying at Jimmy's mom's boyfriend's,

my cousin, he took me out on skateboards,

and I got buzzed. He said, Willie,

Willie, kick with the other leg. And down I went.

On Hillcrest, there you feel free.

I text, much of the night, and follow Iowa south.

MARCH IS THE MADDEST MONTH REFERENCES MARCH MADNESS, A POPULAR COLLEGE BASKETBALL TOURNAMENT.

MUNCHERS IS A 24-HOUR DONUT HOLE-IN-THE-WALL, KNOWN FOR MINI-CINNAMON ROLLS. IN 2013, A MAN WAS ARRESTED HIDING IN THE CEILING OF THE BATHROOM OF MUNCHERS, WAITING FOR IT TO CLOSE SO HE COULD ROB IT. A DREAM DEFERRED.

BLOWN TO "HERE" IS A REFERENCE TO THE HERE APARTMENT COMPLEX, AN EXAMPLE OF LAZY MODERN STUDENT LIVING, WHICH CREATED QUITE A CONTROVERSY FOR ITS DELAYED BEGINNINGS AND ITS PLEDGE TO BRING AN IMAGINARY ROBOTIC PARKING LOT TO THE CITY, WHICH IT NEVER FULFILLED.

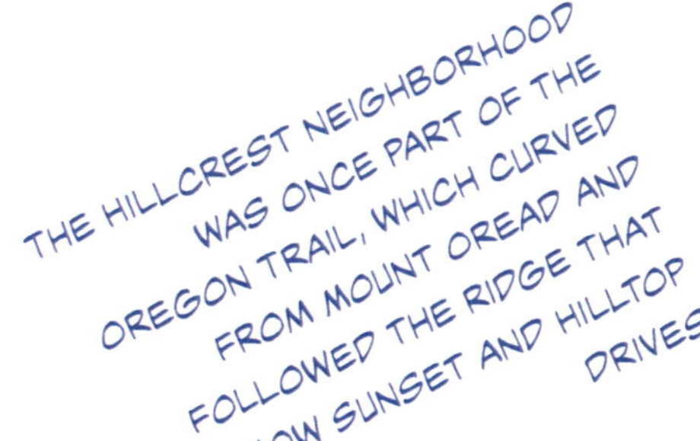

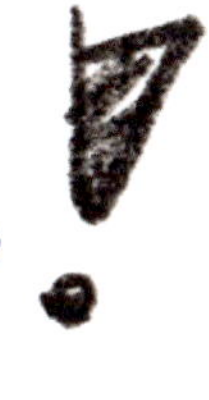

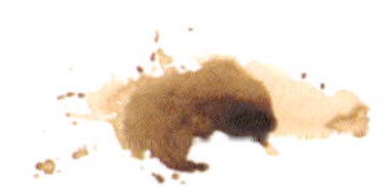

What are the mums that clutch, what tiny trees grow

out of downtown planters? Children of Self,

you cannot say, or guess, for you know only

a heap of dead restaurants, now Starbucks,

and dim downtown gives no shelter, buskers no relief,

and the wading pool no sound of water. Only

there is a plaque on this red rock,

(here much longer than white people this red rock)

and I will show you something different than either

your shadow at Louise's striding behind you

or your shadow at Leroy's rising to meet you.

I will show you fear in a handful of drunks.

Bullwinkle's lit.

Your outfit is fire.

Bitch threw shade.

Weird flex, she thirsty.

"You gave me sunflowers first a year ago;"

"They called me the Sunflower girl."

—Yet, when we came back, late, from Grinter's Farm,

your Instagram full, and your hair wet, I could not

speak, and my iPhone failed, I was neither

living nor dead, and I knew nothing,

looking into the eternal flame, the silence.

Ex cinere ut immortalitatis."

THIS RED ROCK REFERS TO THE SACRED RED ROCK, A LARGE PIECE OF QUARTZITE WHICH WAS PLACED IN A DOWNTOWN PARK BETWEEN THE NORTH LAWRENCE BRIDGES. THE ROCK WAS ORIGINALLY A SACRED PLACE OF WORSHIP BY THE KAW TRIBE, BUT LAWRENCE CITIZENS MADE IT INTO A PLAQUE CELEBRATING THE WHITE SETTLERS OF THE TOWN. IT WAS RETURNED TO THE KAW TRIBE IN 2022, AND REMATRICULATED TO IT'S HONORED PLACE IN COUNCIL GROVE, KANSAS.

HERE THE CALLS MIMIC THE CACOPHONY OF CHATTER ONE MIGHT HEAR IN ONE OF LAWRENCE'S MANY UNDERAGE DRINKING ESTABLISHMENTS.

GRINTER'S FARM IS A POPULAR SUNFLOWER FIELD FOR TAKING PHOTOGRAPHS. THE TRAFFIC BACKUPS ARE LEGENDARY.

EX CINERE UT IMMORTALITATIS-- "FROM ASHES TO IMMORTAILITY," THE MOTTO OF THE CITY OF LAWRENCE. DOWNTOWN LAWRENCE HAS A HISTORY OF BEING SET ON FIRE OR CATCHING ON FIRE SPONTANEOUSLY. THE LANDMARK ELDRIDGE HOTEL HAS CAUGHT FIRE THREE TIMES, LAWRENCE AND FIRE HAVE A THING.

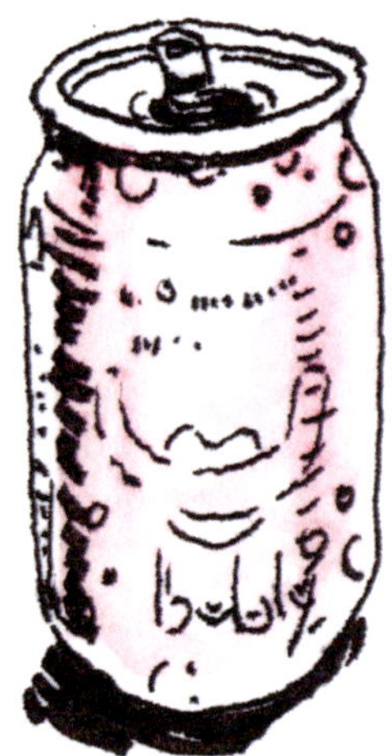

Third Eye Sadie, the village witch,

has a bad cold, nevertheless

is known to be the wisest woman on the North Side

with a wicked pack of cards. Here, said she,

is your card—the drowned Rugby Player.

(Those are beer pong balls that were his eyes. Look!)

Here is Maraca Girl, from

    down the Block,

the lady of lamentations.

Here is the Man in Chainmail

    with three staves, riding by

    The Wheel,

and here is the chef from

    Merchants, and this card,

which is blank, is probably

    a menu for Restaurant Week,

which I am forbidden to attend.

    I do not find

The Tan Man. Fear death by city water.

I see crowds of people, walking round a fountain.

Thank you. If you see dear Mrs. Millstein

tell her I bring the triple latte myself:

one must be so careful these days.

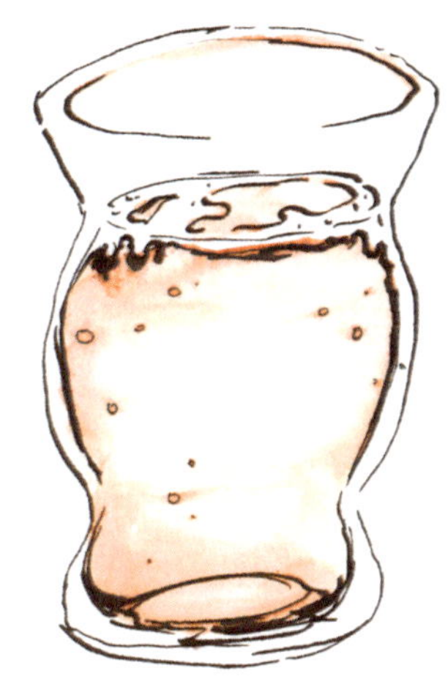

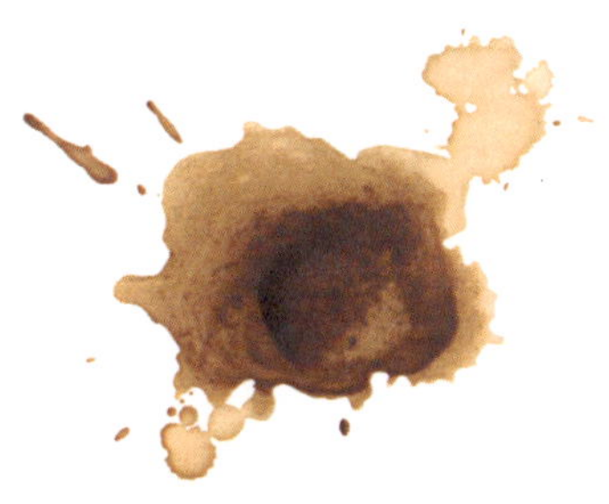

Unreal City,

Beware the Phog as summer dawns,

a crowd flooded over the North Lawrence

bridge, so many

I had not thought the sidewalk sale had undone so many.

Sighs, short and infrequent, were exhales

each person fixed their eyes before their feet

flowed cross the bridge and down Massachusetts Street,

to where the County Hall clock kept the hours

with a dude passed out on the corner of ninth.

There I saw one I knew and stopped him crying: "Auman!

"You who were with me storming downtown after Chalmers shot!"

"That foot you put in a jar on your porch last year,

"has it begun to grow back? Is half Einstein's brain still in your basement?"

"Or has all sense left this goddamn town?"

"Oh keep Missou far hence, that maddens men."

"Or with fresh hope, he'll dig it up again!"

"You! Hypocrite l'accompagnateur—*frere Jayhawk*—*craie de roche*!"

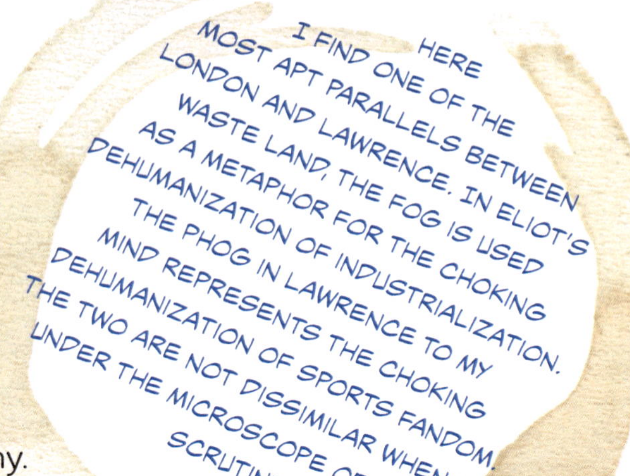

CHALMER'S SHOT:

THE SIDEWALK SALE WAS AN ANNUAL CACOPHONY OF CAPITALISM--THE BEST AND WORST OF LAWRENCE. FROM ABOUT 5 A.M., MERCHANTS PUT THEIR WARES ON THE SIDEWALK AT SMALL DISCOUNTS, ALONG WITH ICED-DOWN TUBS OF BOTTLED WATER, IN THE BLISTERING SUMMER SUN OF KANSAS. HOT AND THIRSTY SHOPPERS WANDERED IN SEARCH OF SOME SMALL DEAL. THE WHOLE THING WAS HORRIFIC AND CHARMING.

TWO ACTUAL THINGS THAT HAPPENED: 1) IN 2005, 21-YEAR OLD EZEKIEL RUBOTTOM HAD HIS AMPUTATED FOOT SEIZED BY POLICE FROM HIS PORCH ON 627 CONNECTICUT STREET WHERE HE HAD IT STORED IN A FIVE-GALLON BUCKET OF FORMALDEHYDE. IT WAS LATER RETURNED TO HIM. 2) FROM 1988 TO 1996 PART OF EINSTEIN'S BRAIN WAS KEPT IN LAWRENCE BY PATHOLOGIST THOMAS HARVEY DURING HIS TIME IN THE CITY.

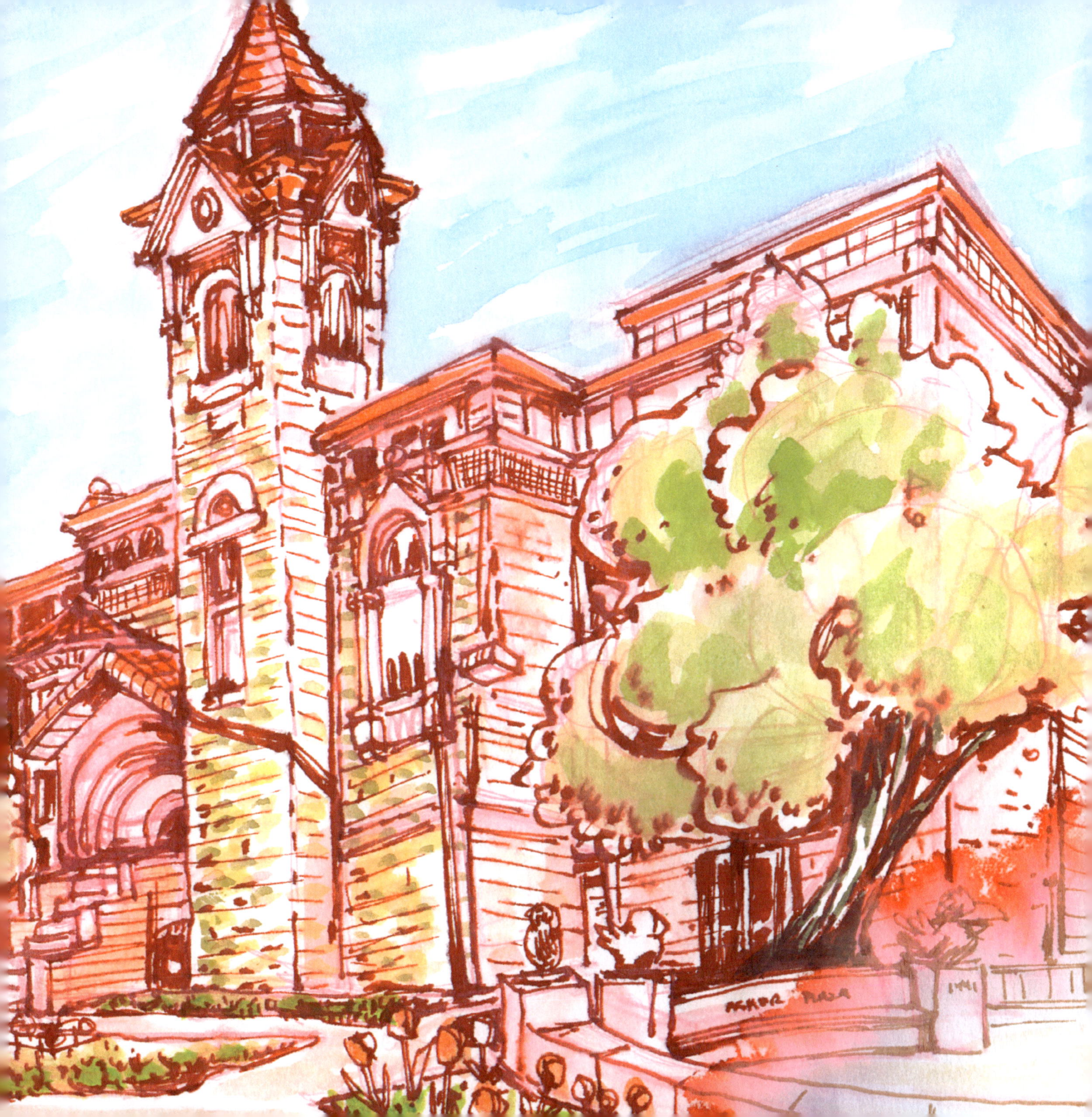

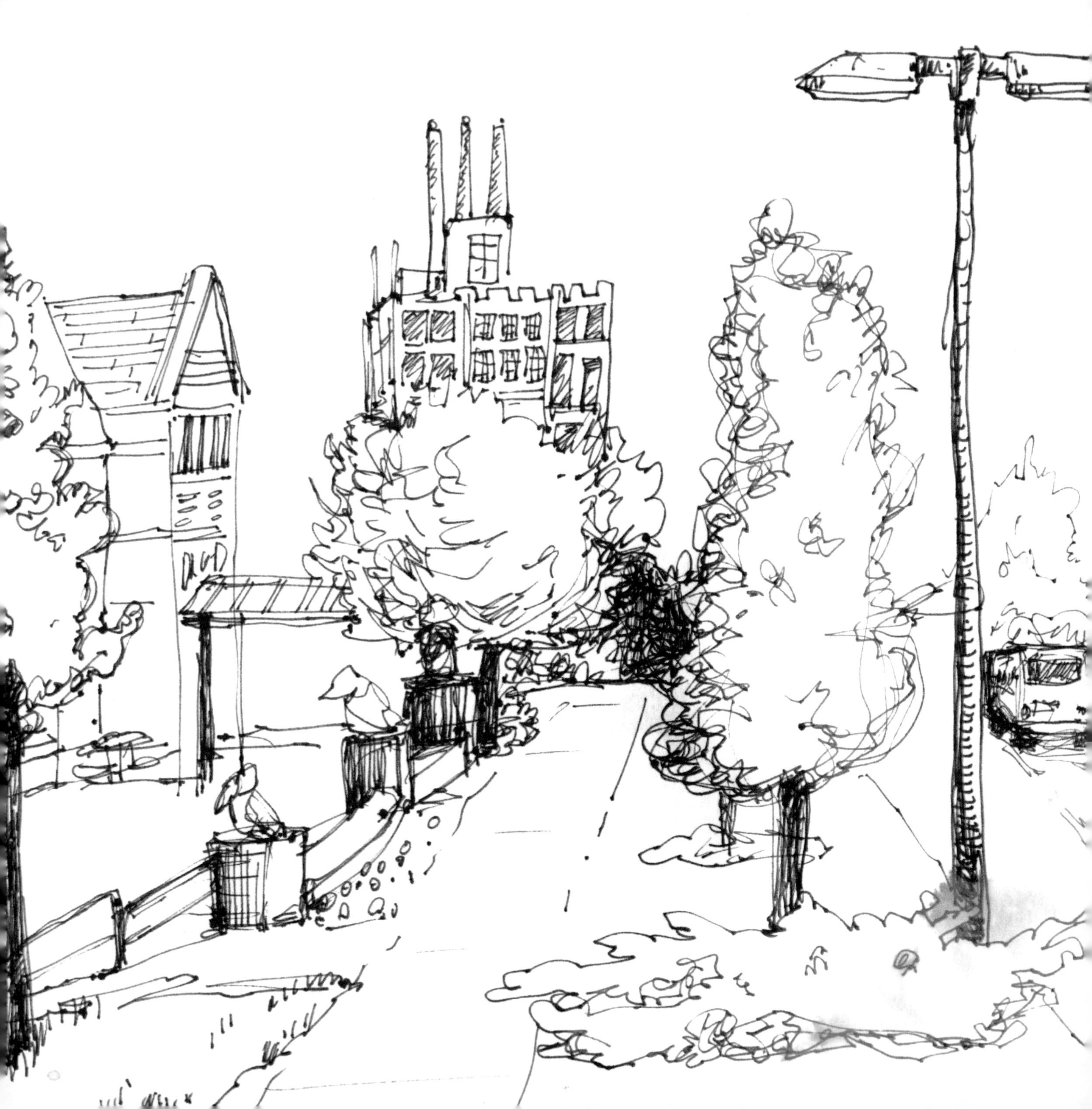

II. A Game of Hoops

The Bench they sat on, like a varnished throne
blanched the wooden floors, where the paint
marked boundaries with curved lines.
In the center a blue Jayhawk peeped out
(Another few looked down from banners on the ceiling)
doubled in intensity by lights from the rows of fluorescents,
reflecting light through the field house as
the squeaking sound of sneakers rose to fill it,
from vinyl-lined chairs sat in rich profusion
in outfits of white with blue lettering,
unstoppable, lurked these lanky, dedicated men.
Forward, Guard, or Center—troubled, confused,
down by ten with four minutes left; stirred by the crowd
that belted from the stands, cheers ascended
full slandering the coach of the other team,
flung their shade onto the visitors
stirring the movement from the other side.
Electric scoreboard ablaze with LED
burned red and blue, framed by ceiling's vaults
from which dim light, some jerseys hang

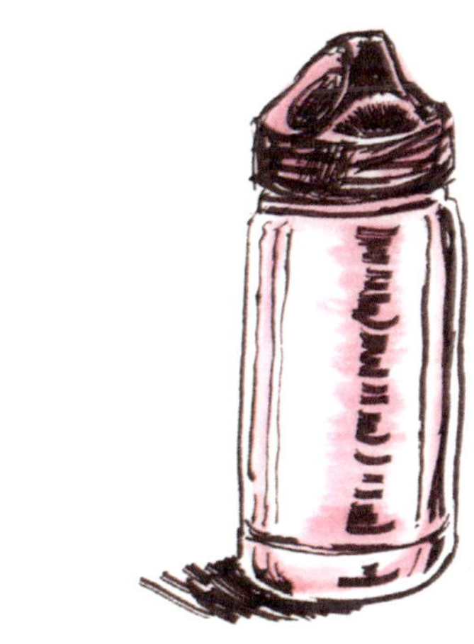

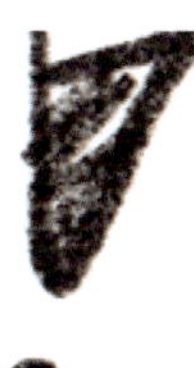

and above the crowd's north side, a sign was displayed:

Pay Heed All Who Enter, BEWARE OF THE PHOG.

the temple of Naismith, the Basketball King

so blessedly inspired, and there his game

filled all the Fieldhouse with inviolable voice

and still they cry, and still the world pursues,

"Jay, Jay, Jayhawk" to dirty ears.

And other long-gone championships

were told upon the banners; sentinel forms

hanging, majestic, hushing the room enclosed.

Footsteps squealed endlessly upon the floor

under the bright light, under the scoreboard,

his hands

wrapped each other as he sat

while others got minutes, still he sat savagely still.

"I am fucking tripping balls. Yes, balls. Stay with me.

"Speak to me. Why do you never speak? Speak.

"Do you want tacos? Which taco? What?

"I might throw up over here, OK?"

I think we are in the Eighth Street alley

where Cielito Lindo dumps its grease.

IT IS IMPOSSIBLE TO DENY THE ARENA-AS-CATHEDRAL AIR THAT PERMEATES ALLEN FIELD HOUSE. EVEN A CYNICAL POET CANNOT HELP BUT APPRECIATE THE RITUAL AND HISTORY ATTACHED TO THIS SPACE.

I HAVE ALWAYS HAD GREAT EMPATHY FOR SECOND AND THIRD-STRING PLAYERS WHO SPEND THEIR COLLEGE EXPERIENCE RIDING THE PINE. IT MUST BE EXTRAORDINARILY FRUSTRATING TO BE SO CLOSE TO YOUR DREAM, YET FORCED TO SIT ON THE SIDELINES, WATCHING, UNTIL THE SCORE HAS GROWN SO ONE-SIDED YOU'RE THROWN IN FOR THE LAST FIVE MINUTES.

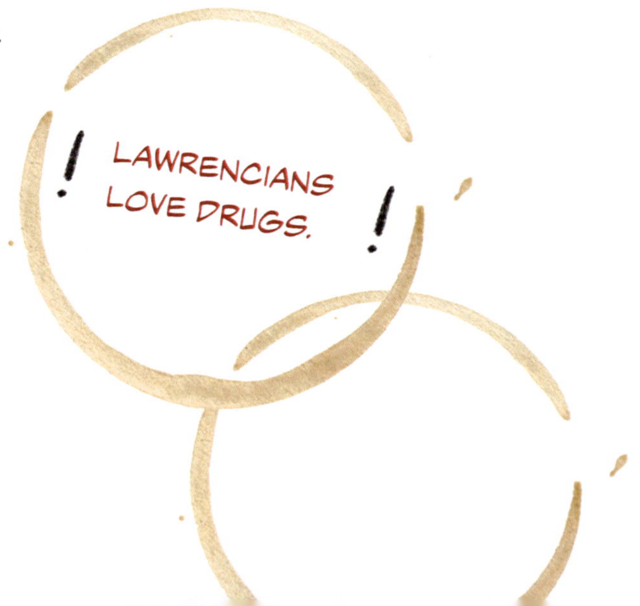

THE ALLEY ON 8TH AND MASS HAS A SMELL ONE DOES NOT FORGET.

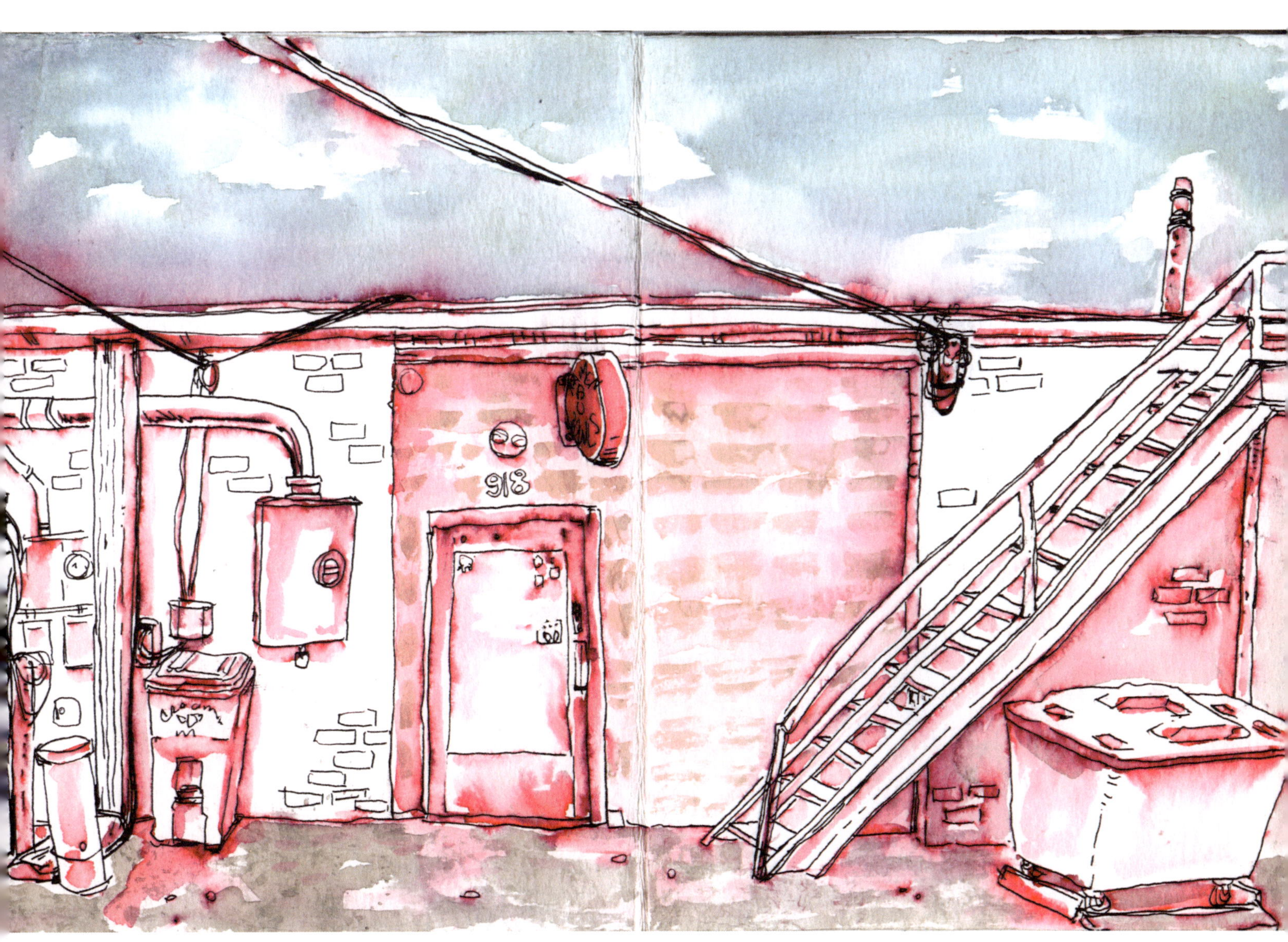
918

"What is that noise?"

      "They're waiting for the Sandbar,"

"What is that noise now? What are they doing?"

     Flirting drunkly flirting

        "Did

you try flirting? Did you fail flirting? Do you win

flirting?"

  I remember

those beer pong balls that were his eyes

"Are you hot or not? Are you seeing anyone?"

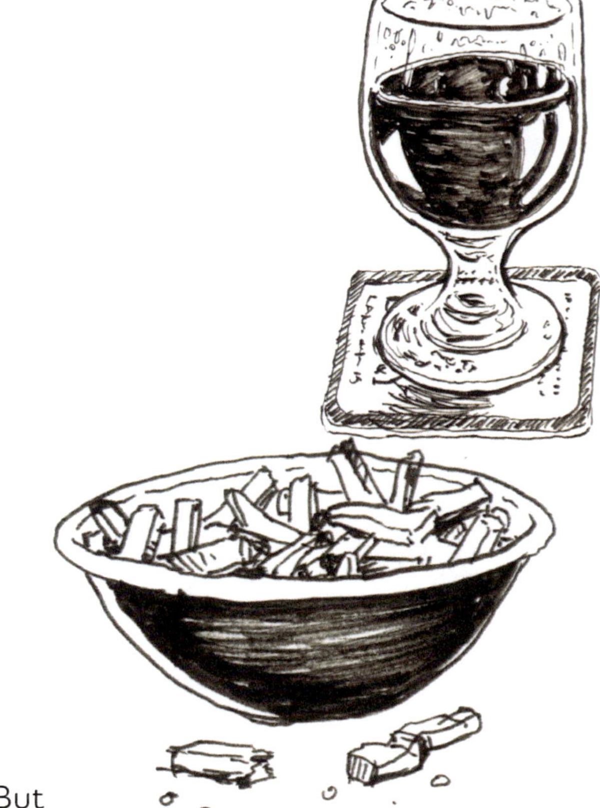

                   But

O O O O that Public Librarheian Rag— 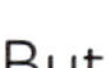

it's all around

Heart of Downtown

"Where should we eat now? What should we do?"

"I just gotta grab a coat, then hit the street."

"Your hair, wear this hat, so. What should we do tonight?"

"What shall we ever do?"

THE MISSPELLING HERE IS INTENTIONAL--ELIOT REFERS TO A "SHAKESPEHERIAN RAG" IN THE ORIGINAL POEM, JUXTAPOSING THE ELOQUENCE OF SHAKESPEARE'S WORK WITH THE ROUGH BROGUE OF LONDON GIN-JOINT DRINKERS. THE PARALLELS TO THE LIBRARY SEEMED APT IN LIGHT OF THIS, AS A GATHERING POINT AND SOCIAL HUB OF DOWNTOWN.

                They stop serving food at ten-thirty

and if we close it, after-party till four

and we shall play a game of hoops

or Madden, rip bong hits, wait for a knock upon the door.

When Chrissy's husband got fired for doing coke in the walk-in—

I didn't mince words, I said to her myself-

LAST CALL FOR ALCOHOL

now Vaughn's coming back, put some pants on.

he'll want to know what you did with that forty dollars

for the whitening strips. Remember, the Crest.

To whiten your teeth. He did, I was there—

    You have to get like thirty, Chrissy, don't get generic

he said, I swear, and left, he said, for the Replay.

I'm all like, he's right, and think of poor Vaughn,

    He's been in the service industry for ten years, he wants a good time,

    and if you don't give it to him, there's others that will, I said.

    Fuck you, she said. If he wants to, I said.

    Then I'll know who to thank, she said, and ordered more wings.

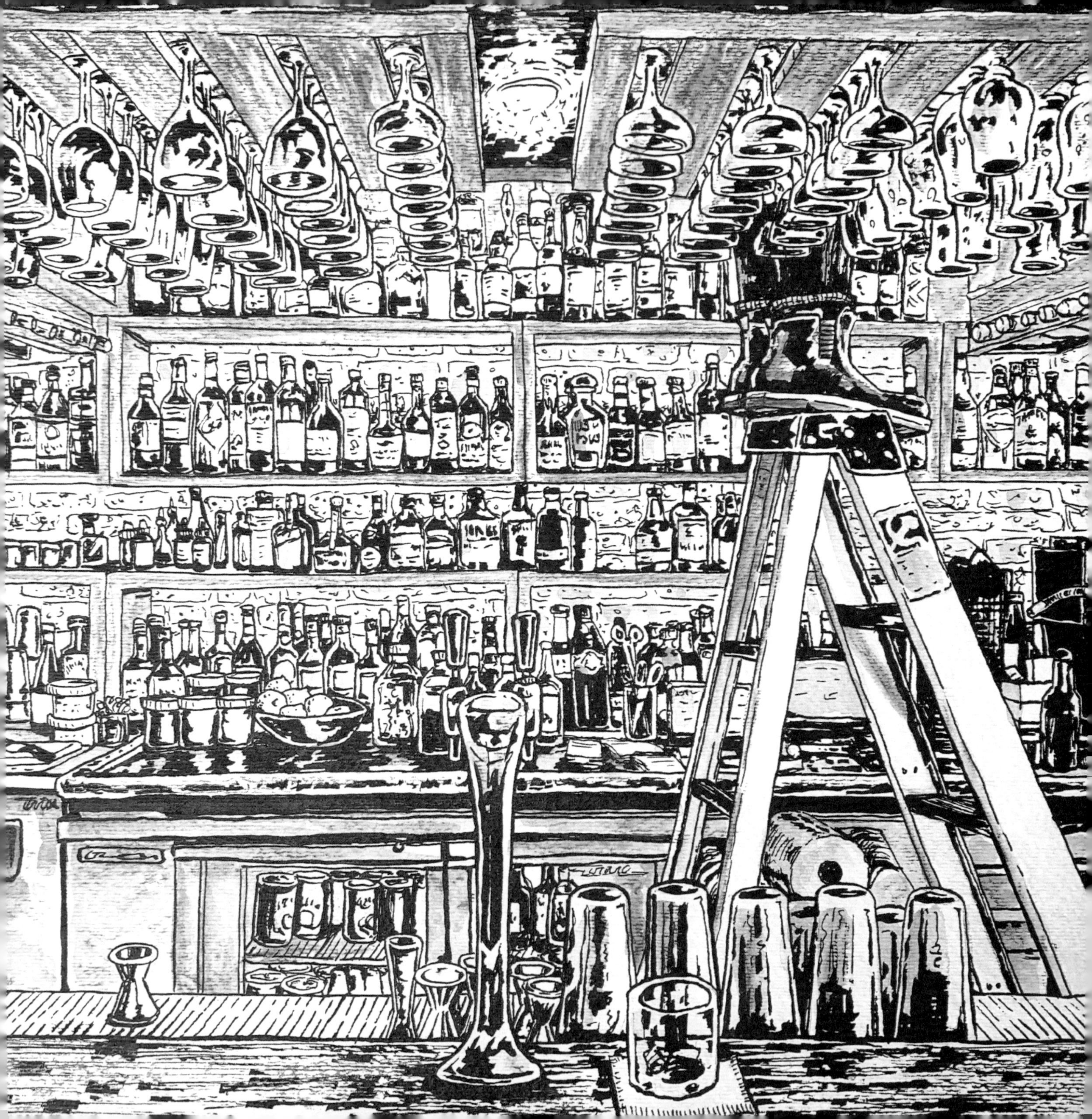

LAST CALL FOR ALCOHOL

If you don't like it, just go, I said.

Others can pick and choose if you can't.

But if Vaughn takes off, it won't be for lack of telling.

It will be for those nasty-ass teeth, I said, you look like shit.

(She's like thirty-one.)

It's not my fault, she goes, makes this face,

It's these kombuchas I drink and the meth to keep an edge. The dogs

(she's adopted five already, every Humane Society appeal)

the guy at the Merc said I'd be fine, but I've never been the same.

You are a fucking dummy, I said.

But, if Vaughn won't let up, just give in, I said,

what you live together for if you don't want dogs?

LAST CALL FOR ALCOHOL

Well, that Sunday Vaughn was home, they had some smoked brisket,

and they asked me to dinner, and you don't say no to that–

LAST CALL FOR ALCOHOL

LAST CALL, LAST CALL FOR ALCOHOL

Goonight, Adri. Goonight, Kitty. Goonight, Nikol. Goonight.

See ya! Goonight. Goonight.

Good night, people, good night, fuck y'all I'm out, good night.

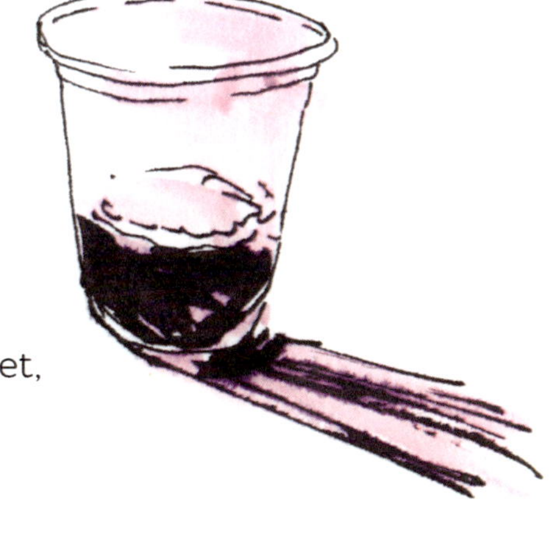

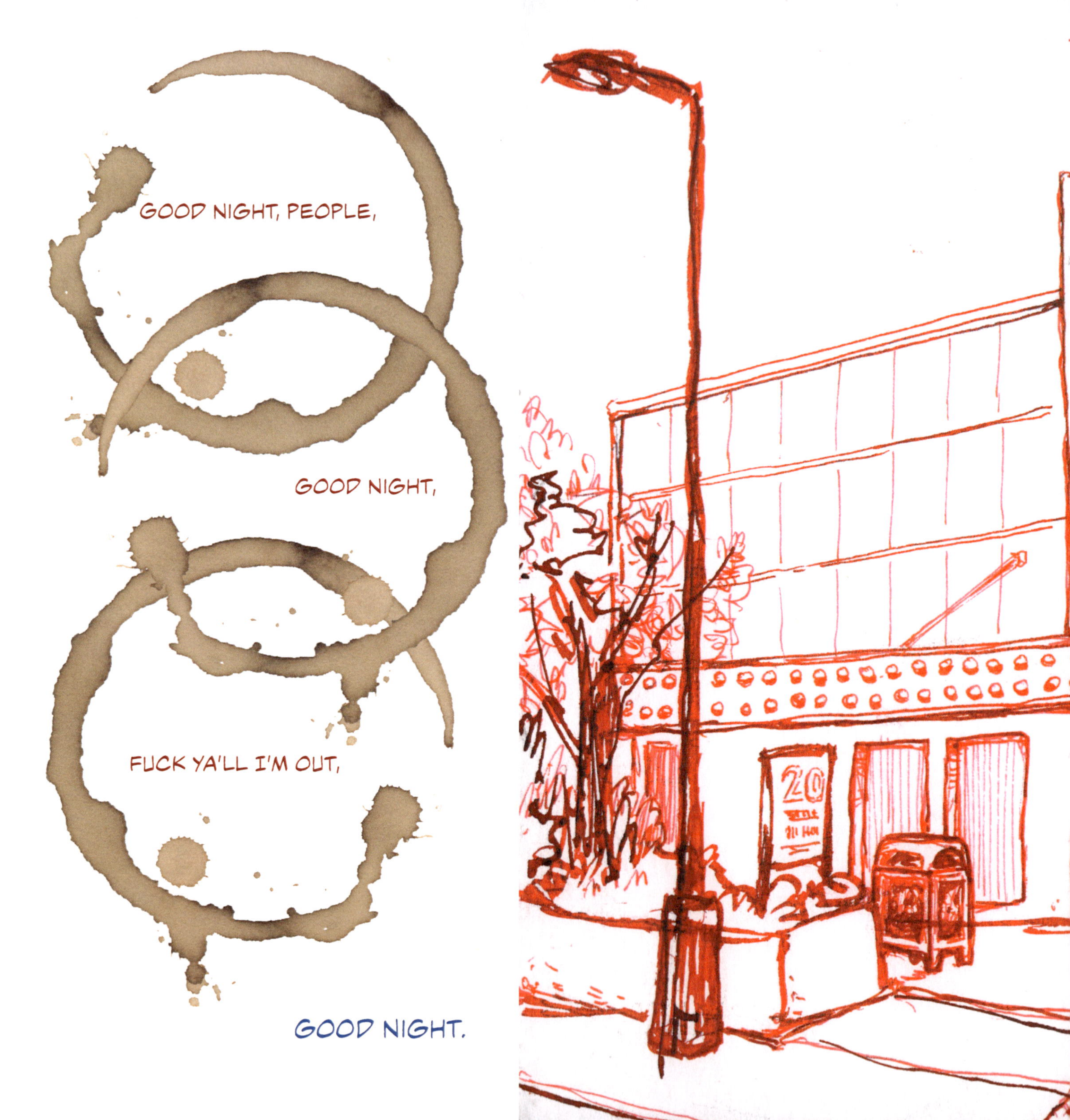
GOOD NIGHT, PEOPLE,
GOOD NIGHT,
FUCK YA'LL I'M OUT,
GOOD NIGHT.

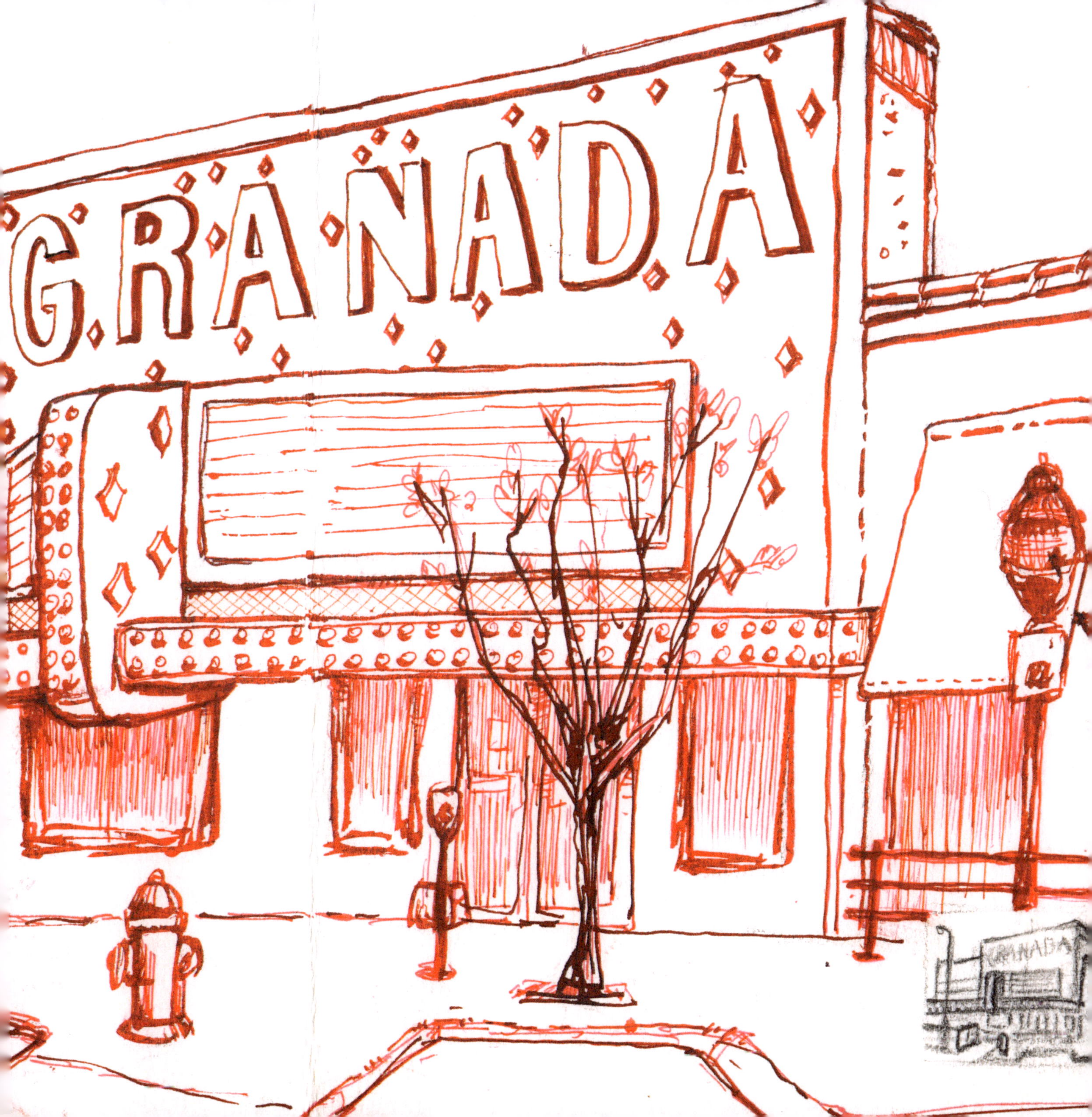

G. RAÑADA
GRANADA

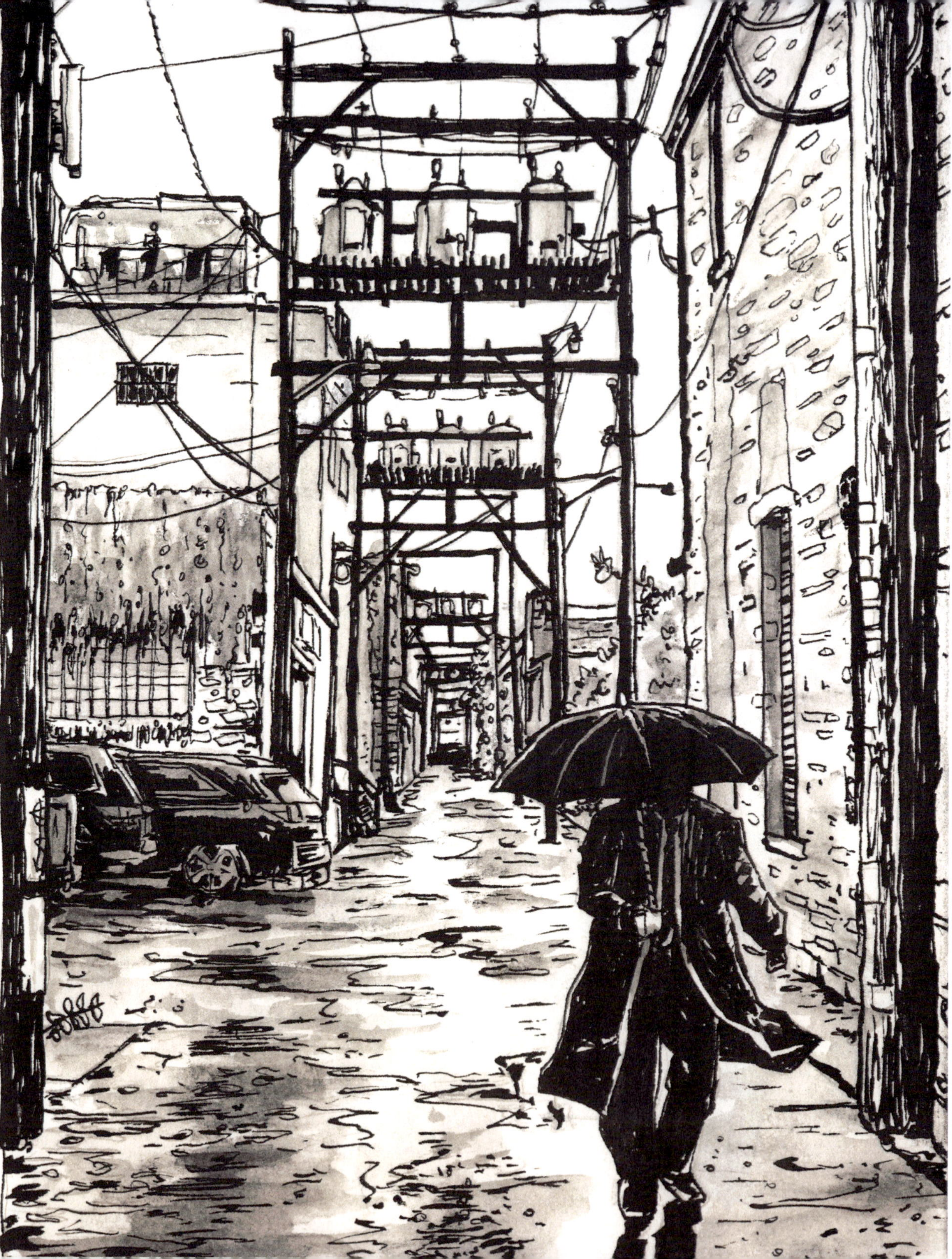

III. Quantrill's Sermon

Broken tents line the river: skeletal fingers

of aluminum, clutch into the wet bank. The wind

crosses the mudlands, unheard. Precious Love gone west.

Sweet Kaw, run softly, till I end my song.

The river bears no beer cans, Whopper wrappers,

disposable masks, six-pack holders, underwear

or other testimony of summer nights. Precious Love gone west.

And his friends, loitering troupes of downtown day players,

departed, took carts and left.

By the waters of Potter's Lake I sat down and wept…

Sweet Kaw, run softly to the end of my song.

Sweet Kaw, run softly, for I speak not loud or long.

Across the bridge in a cold blast I hear

North Wind rattlin', highways spread ear-to-ear.

Opossum lumbered down the bank,

dragging its fat belly through mud,

while I was fishing on the jetty

on a winter evening, behind the Gaslight.

Musing upon the Provost, my brother's, wreck

and upon the Provost, my father's, death before him.

Houseless bodies strewn across the bank

Native bones cast in a little dry garret,

Rattled by opossum's drunk-alley march,

but at my back from time to time I hear

the silent sounds of used Priuses, which shall bring

Quantrill for his blood in the spring.

Kansas moon shone bright

on James Lane

and his daughter

they wash their feet in Free State beer.

Et O ces voix d'enfants, Agiter le blé! Agiter le blé!

JAMES LANE HID DURING QUANTRILL'S RAID IN A CORNFIELD. EVENTUALLY, HE TURNED CONSERVATIVE AND RACIST AND SHOT HIMSELF. WAS ANYONE FROM THAT TIME A HERO?

Fuck Fuck Fuck

Chug Chug Chug Chug Chug Chug

Jayhawks Heart Consent

Teru.

"THE VOICES OF CHILDREN CRY, "WAVE THE WHEAT. WAVE THE WHEAT." WHEAT, HOPS, AND WATER ARE ALL ESSENTIAL INGREDIENTS IN BEER, WHICH IS DRUNK IN LARGE QUANTITIES DURING BASKETBALL SEASON.

Unreal City

Under white blanket of a winter noon

Kurt Cobain, agony merchant

unshaven, with a pocket full of heroin

plane ticket QR still on his phone

asks me in that Seattle way

to lunch at 715

followed by a Royals game with Burroughs.

KURT COBAIN, GRUNGE KING, ALONG WITH MICHAEL STIPE AND OTHER COUNTER-CULTURE FIGURES, CAME AT SEPARATE TIMES ON PILGRIMAGE TO SEEK OUT WILLIAM BURROUGHS. THEY WOULD GET HIGH AND SHOOT GUNS. BURROUGHS IS ONE OF LAWRENCE'S BEST-KNOWN LITERARY FIGURES AND SHOT HIS WIFE IN THE HEAD IN MEXICO. PEOPLE STILL DIG HIM, THOUGH.

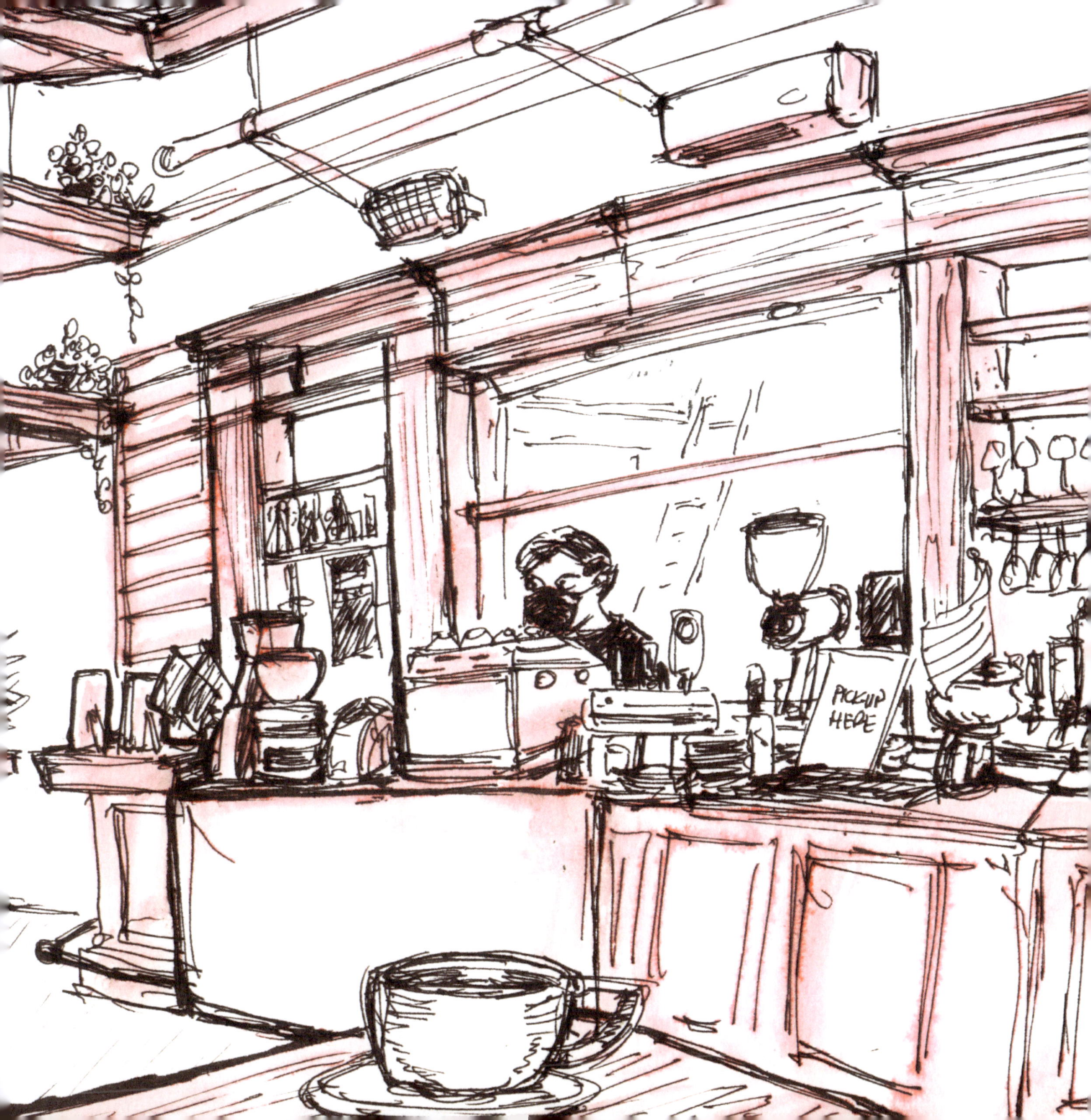

PICK UP HERE

At the gloaming hour, when the eyes

list from screens to windshields, when the human engine idles

like an Uber unseen.

I, John Brown, ever angry, cry havoc between two arms

grizzled bearded white man packing heat, can see

at the gloaming, the evening hour that strives

homeward, dumps commuters off Seventy,

the intern from Callahan heats up Market Fresh chicken, powers

microwave, rips plastic from plastic.

On windows ledge perilously balance

potted herbs, touched by the last rays.

On the duvet are piled (at night her bed)

stockings, slippers, bras, and boots.

I, John Brown, unforgiving and angry

perceived this scene, and foretold the rest—

I awaited with open arms the expected guest.

He, (*new phone, who dis?*) carbuncular, arrives

this guy calls outbound at Maximus, with glassy stare,

one of the low on who assurance sits

as the visor on an Alvamar golfer.

The time is now propitious, as he guesses,

the food's gone cold, she is bold and tired,

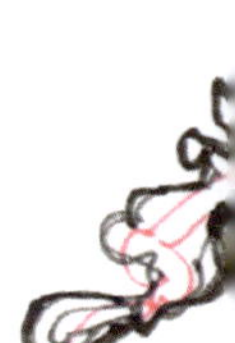

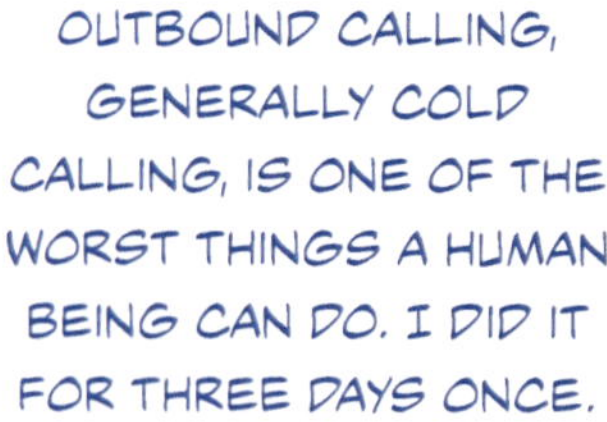

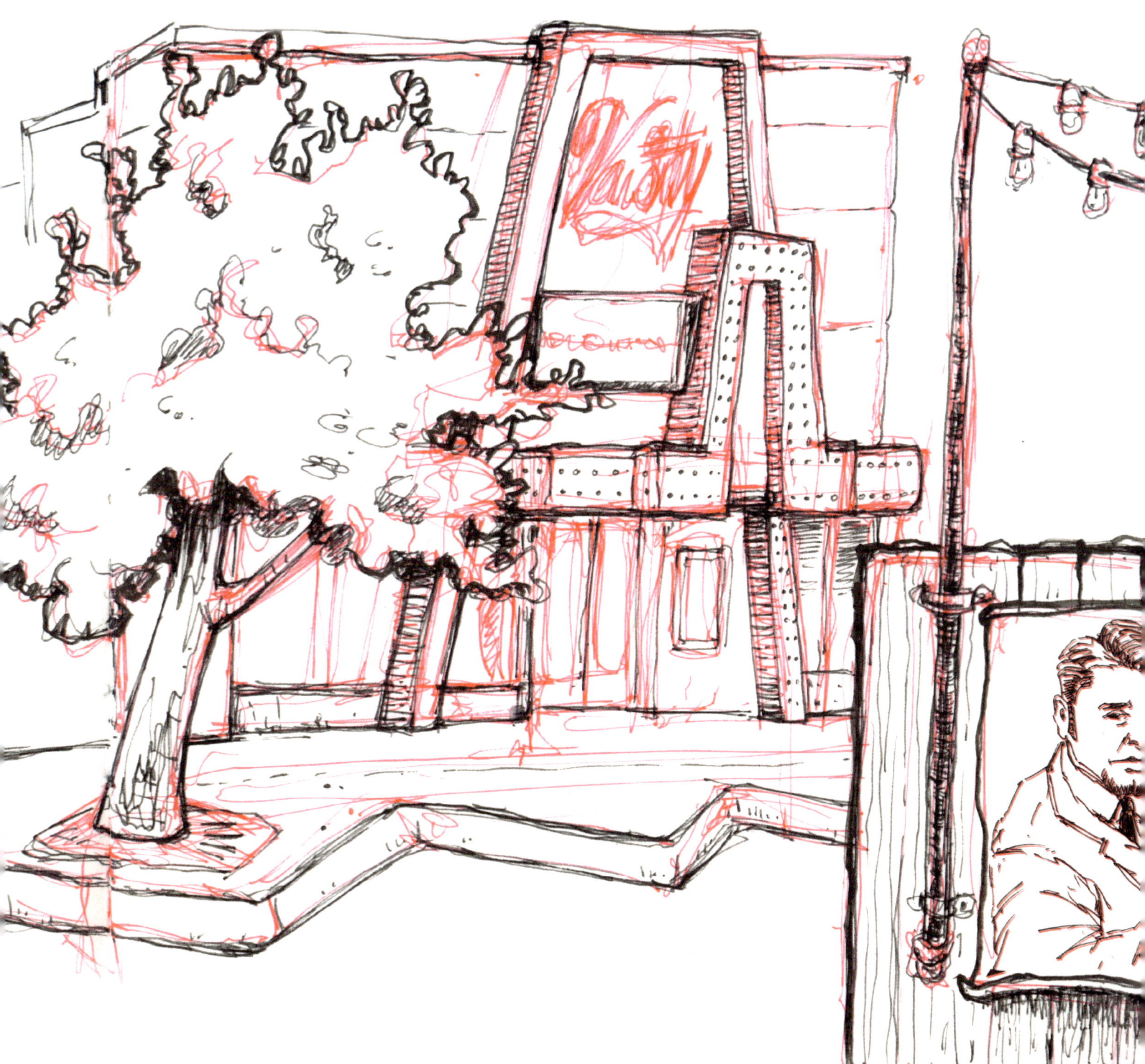
Variety

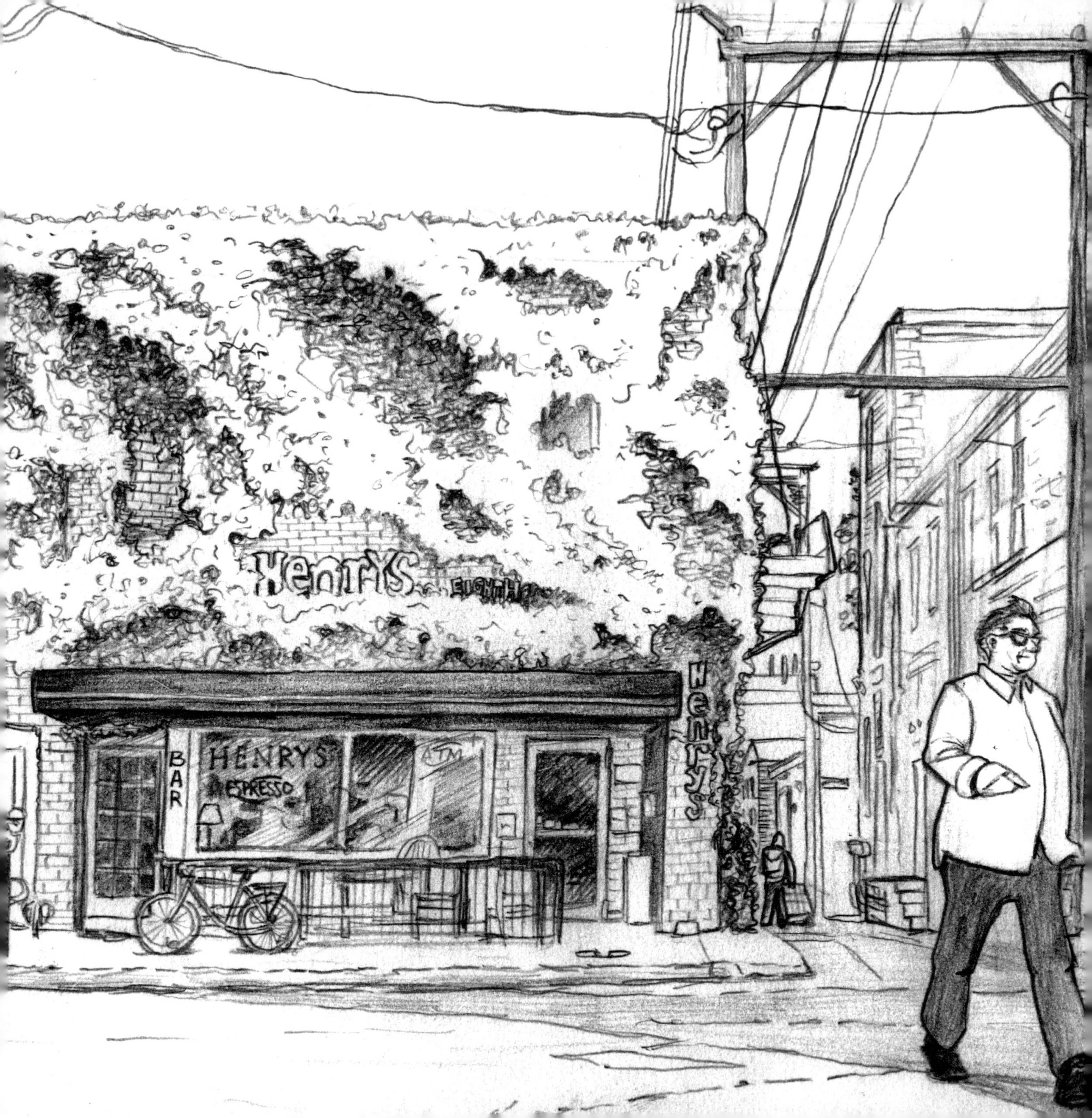
HenryS EIGHTH
Henrys
BAR
HENRYS
ESPRESSO
ATM

endeavors to get a hand down her shirt,

which, I guess, he's not getting slapped for,

Flushed and decided, he shoots his shot,

exploring hands encounter no defense;

his vanity requires no response

and makes a welcome of indifference.

(I, John Brown, have seen it all play out

on this bed or another in this town

I, who am painted on the Capitol wall,

and walked among the lowest of the dead.)

Bestows one final patronizing kiss

and gropes his way, the stairs smell of piss.

She turns and checks herself out in the mirror,

hardly aware that dude took off,

her brain allows one half-formed thought to pass:

"Well, that's done, and I'm glad it's over."

Paces about her room again alone,

she smooths her hair with automatic hand

The Office is on Netflix for one more week.

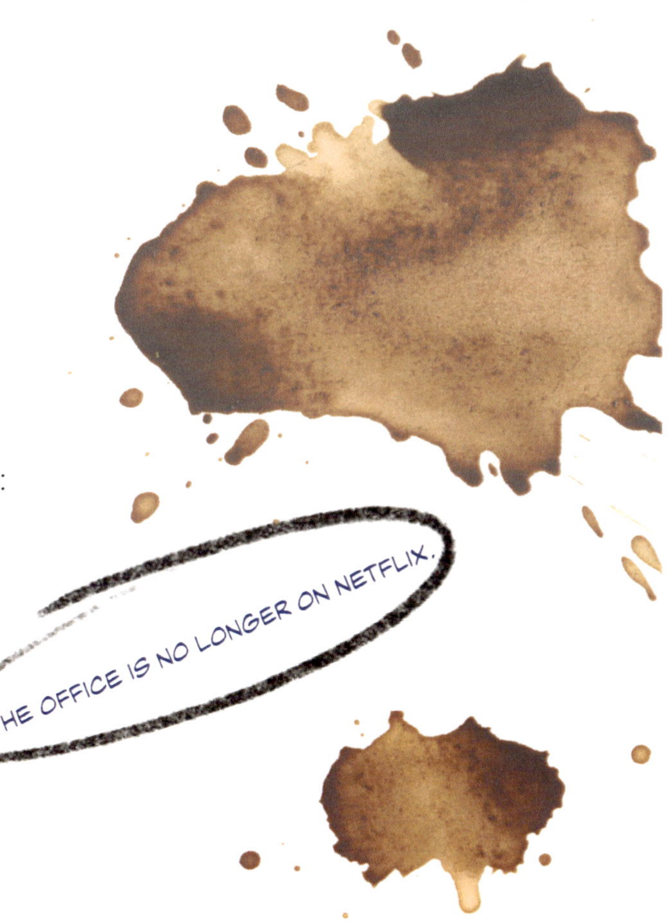

"Raised in the middle of the land full of bar-b-que stands and the brothers throw hands/Everybody grittin gettin grands/Kansas City where the pretty women make you say damn!"

And astride downtown,

on New Hampshire Street,

O City, city, I can sometimes hear

beside the Taproom on Eight Street

the pleasant whining of an accordion

and clatter and a chatter from within

where grad students lounge at noon; where the walls

of Hobbs-Taylor hold

inexplicable splendor in porous rock.

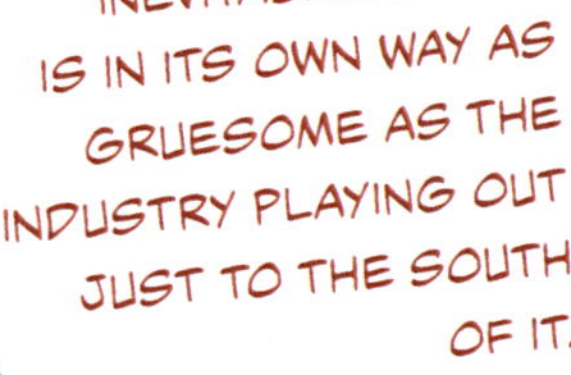

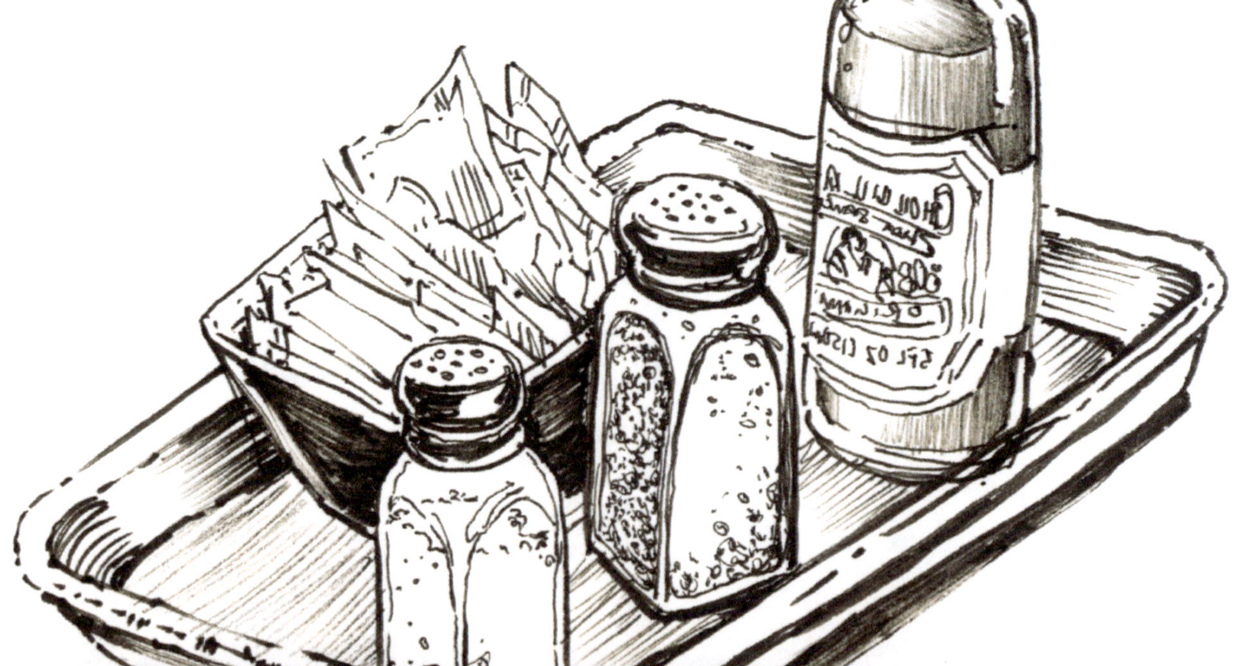

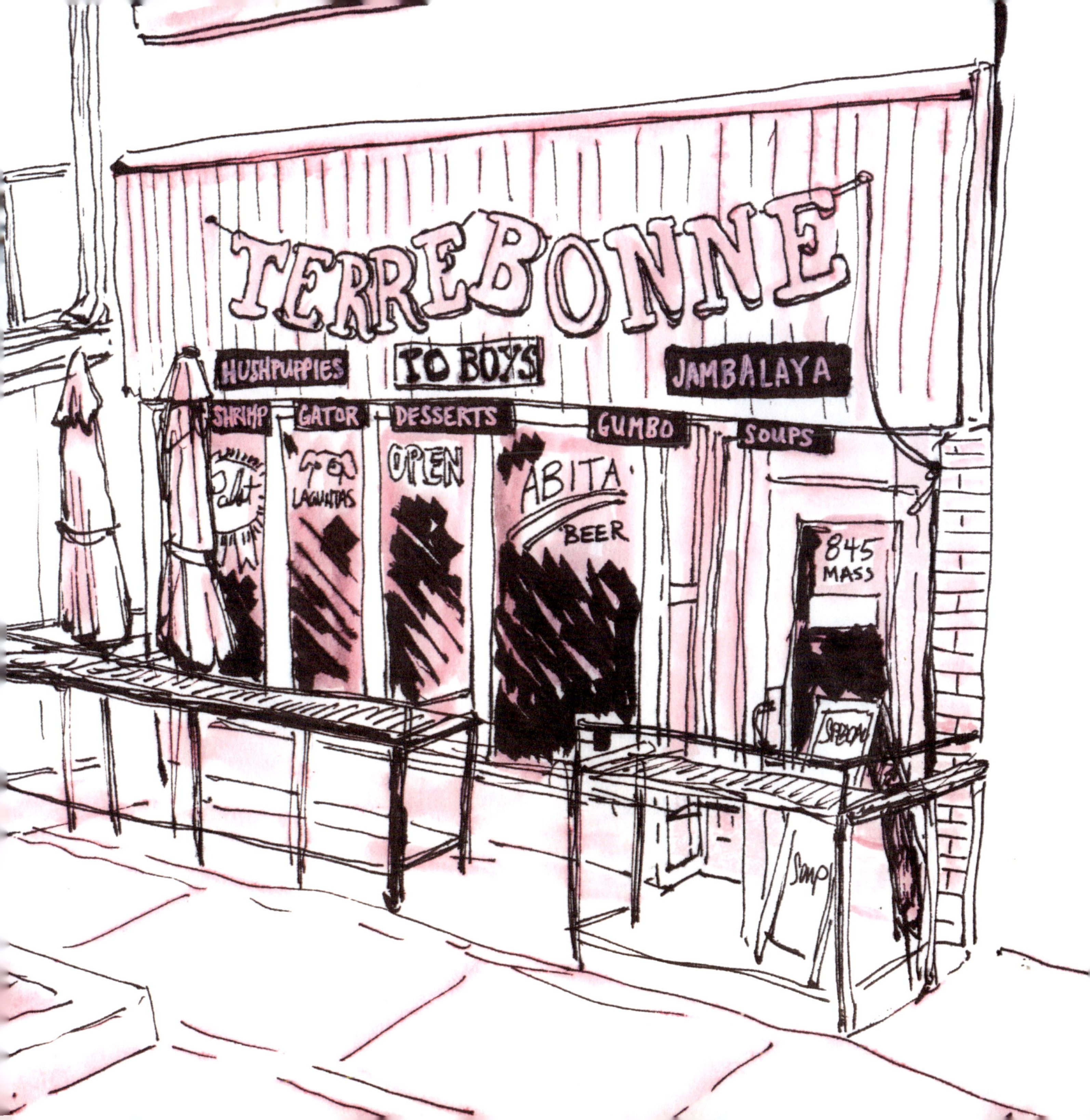

TERREBONNE
HUSHPUPPIES
PO BOYS
JAMBALAYA
SHRIMP
GATOR
DESSERTS
GUMBO
SOUPS
OPEN
LAGUNITAS
ABITA
BEER
845
MASS
SOUP

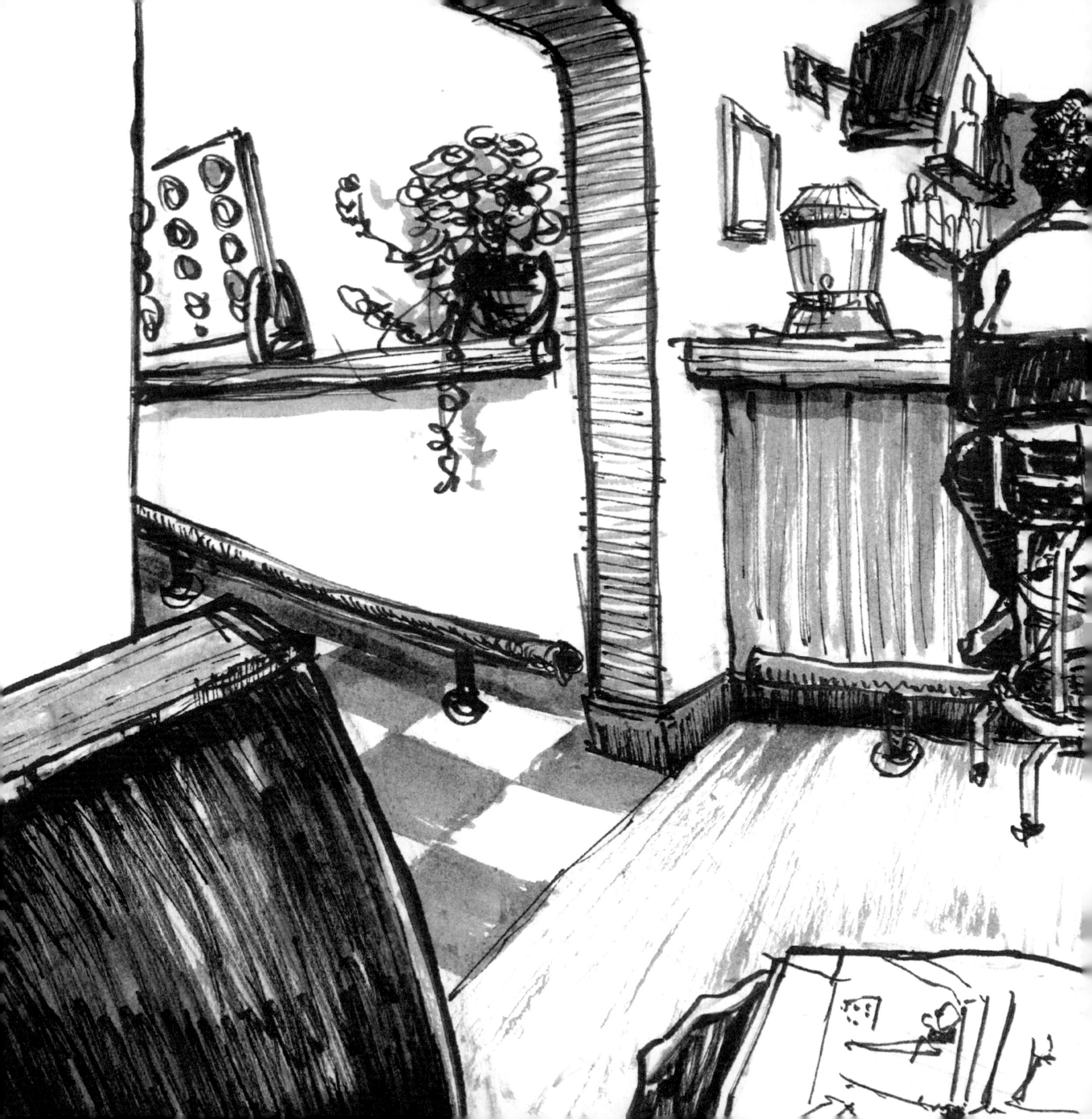

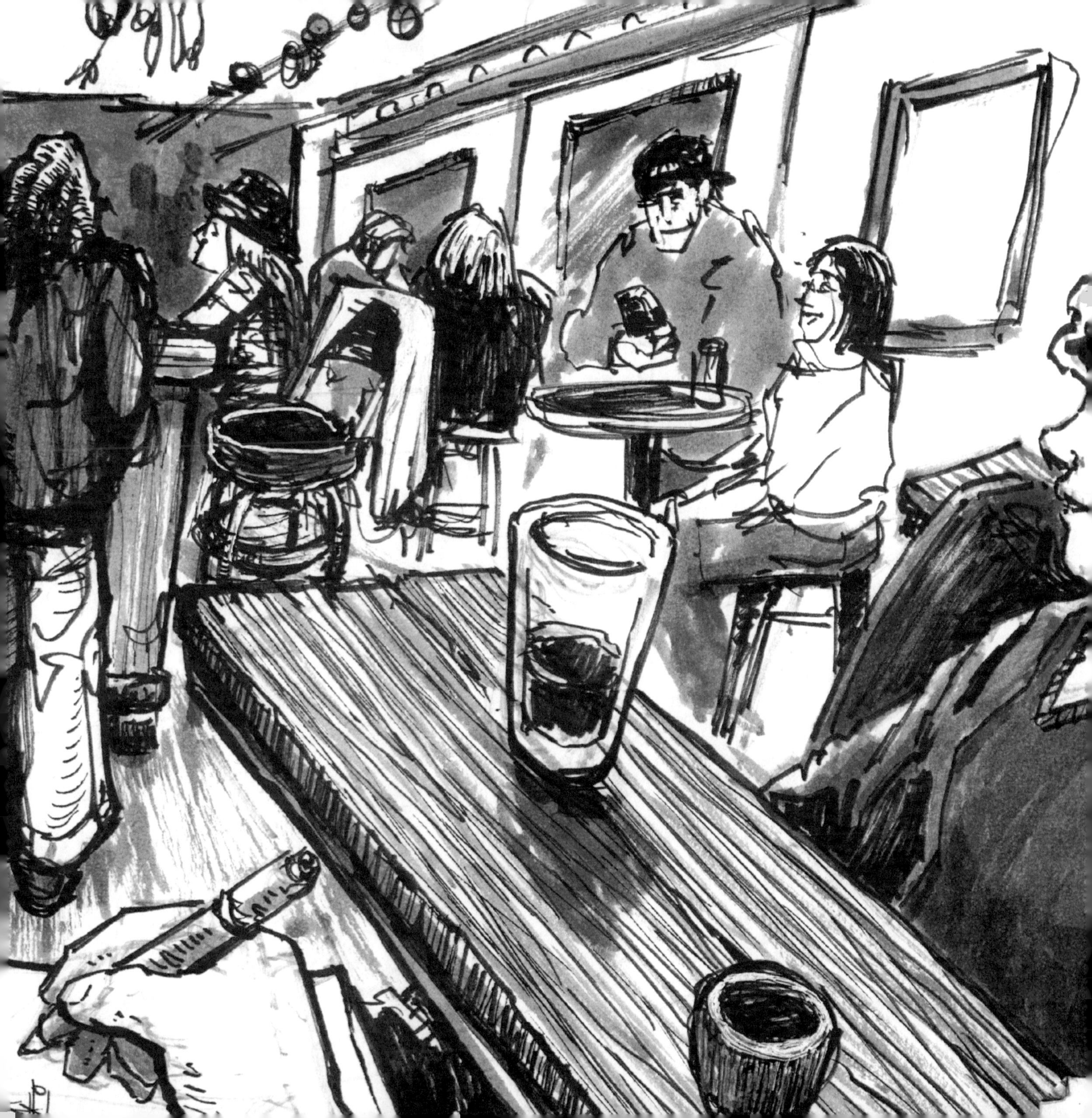

The river sweats

sewage and oil

the trains roll

 in the night their horns

 blast

 Union Pacific

 gone East with coal

 drifting logs,

butt up on Bowersock reach

 up and over to

 rock

 islands below.

 Jessica's on a kayak

 up the river some

 the water moves quickly now

 a good workout

 if you don't

 mind smelling.

Across the river

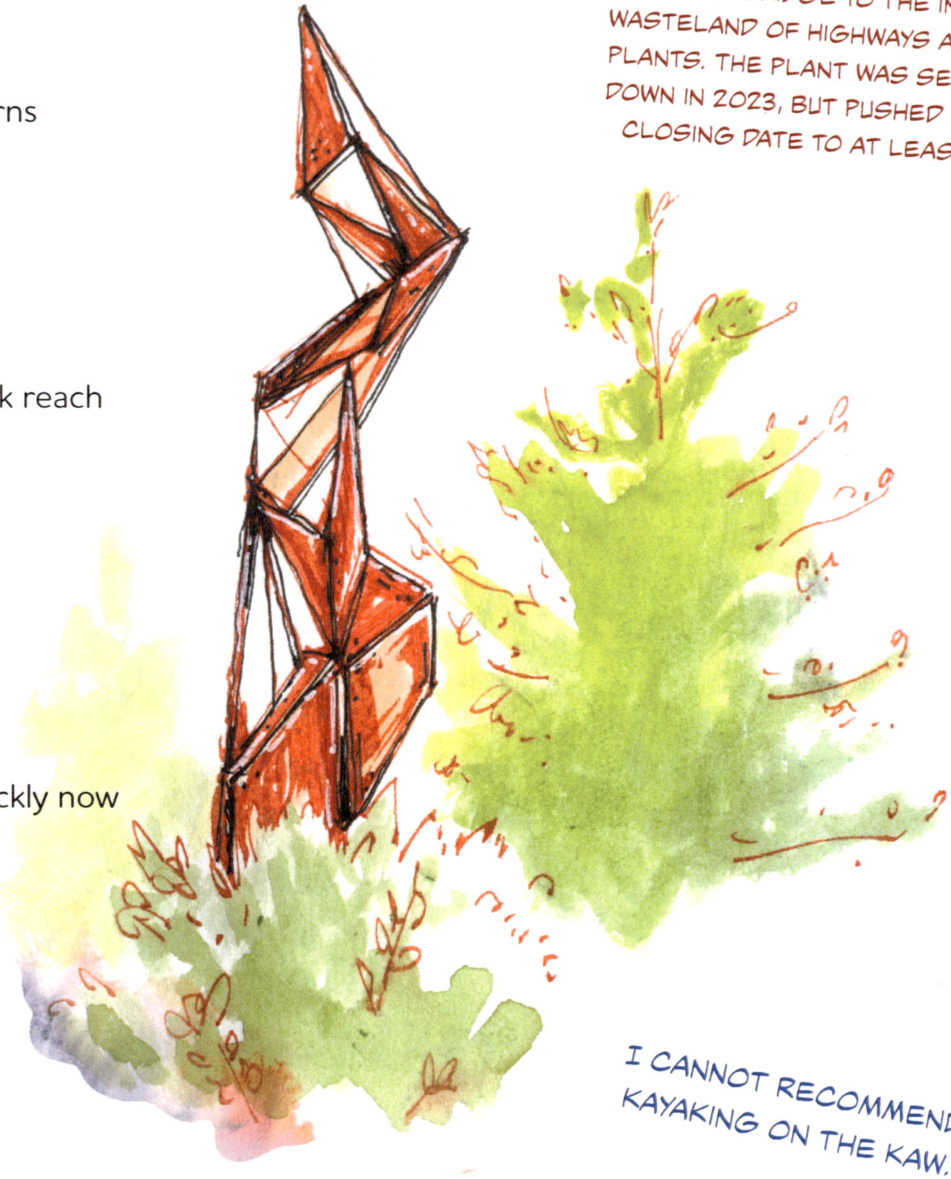

Lost City

of the houseless

gray towers

fabric and aluminum.

THE "T" IS THE NICKNAME FOR LAWRENCE'S BUS TRANSPORTATION. DESPITE IT BEING A MODEL OF EGALITARIAN AFFORDABLE TRANSPORT, IT IS LARGELY UNDERUTILIZED AND DERIDED.

"I took the T and it

took me all day to get from there.

Undid me. By Kasold my headphones stopped.

I looked out in silence."

By Burger King

it looked like smoke

the cars did not stop

I wonder do they care at all

or is this all

flame-broiled now.

THE SIXTH STREET BURGER KING HAS NOT SUCCESSFULLY DELIVERED AN ORDER SINCE ITS BEGINNINGS IN THE MID-SEVENTIES. IT WAS THE SOURCE OF SOME SOCIAL MEDIA CONTROVERSY IN 2022 WHEN A CUSTOMER TOOK SEVERAL PHOTOS OF EMPLOYEES HANGING OUT AND CHATTING, ONE WITH THEIR SHOES OFF, WHILE A LINE OF CUSTOMERS BUILT UP. IF "LORD OF THE FLIES" WAS A FAST-FOOD RESTAURANT, IT WOULD BE THE 6TH STREET BURGER KING.

      La La

AUSTIN HERE SERVES AS THE NATURAL END POINT FOR LAWRENCE. AUSTIN IS LIKE LAWRENCE ELEVATED. AUSTIN > LAWRENCE > PORTLAND, ON THE 2000'S HIPNESS SCALE. AND THEN CAME JOE ROGAN.

      To Austin then I came.

Burning rubber burning engine burning man burning van

O Lord, Gimmie one more gig.

O Lord, just one

Burning

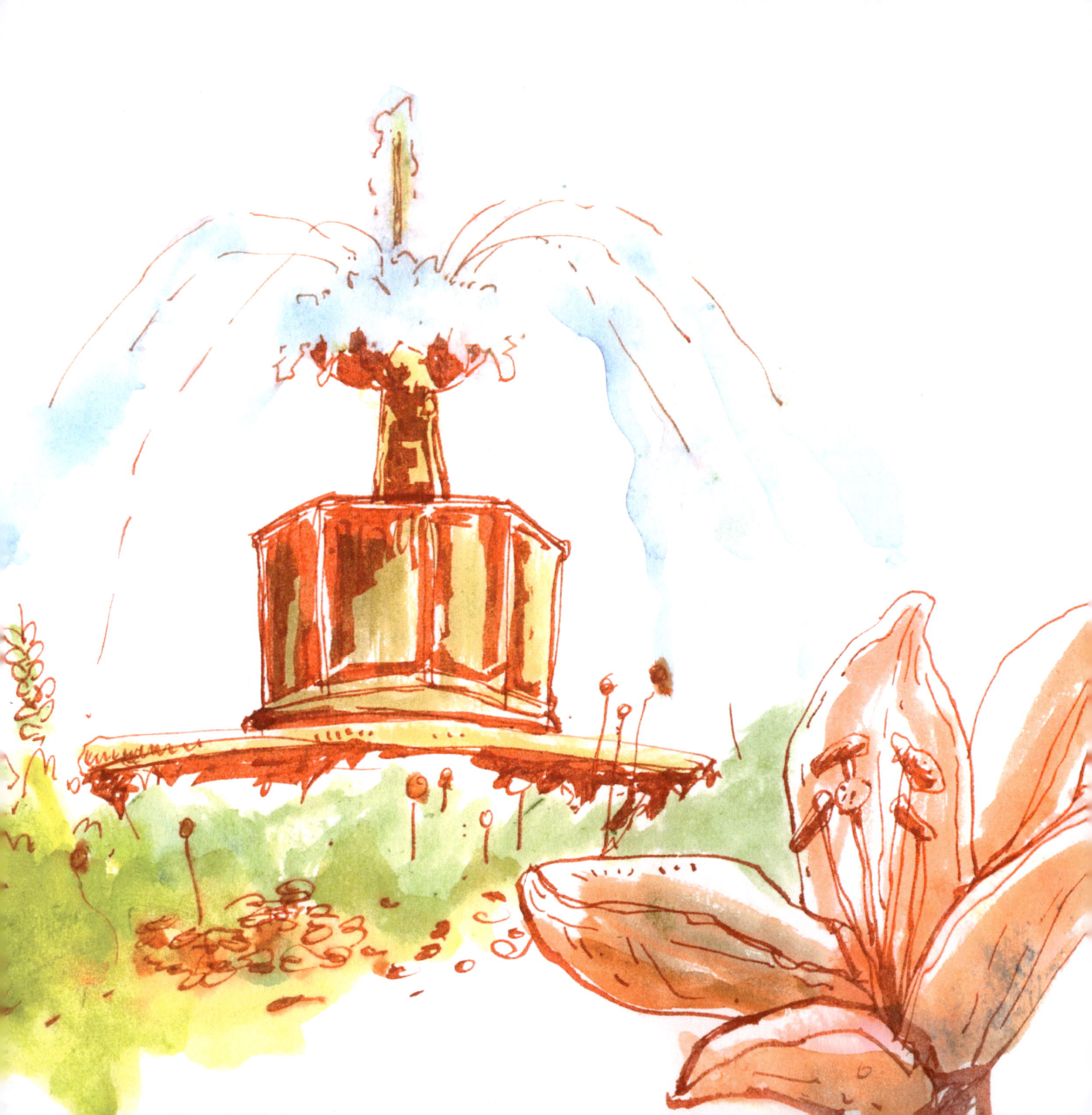

IV. Death by Football

Mark Mangino,

the big guy? He's been gone years.

They say he tried to eat the team,

say he forgot how to play,

I say he never knew.

They blame him

for the fucking disaster on the hill.

but he held that shit together

better than some.

       I don't care who you are

if you don't like college sports,

fuck you. Get the fuck out of here.

Leave under the giant legs of Danny Manning,

spreading west, to the sun.

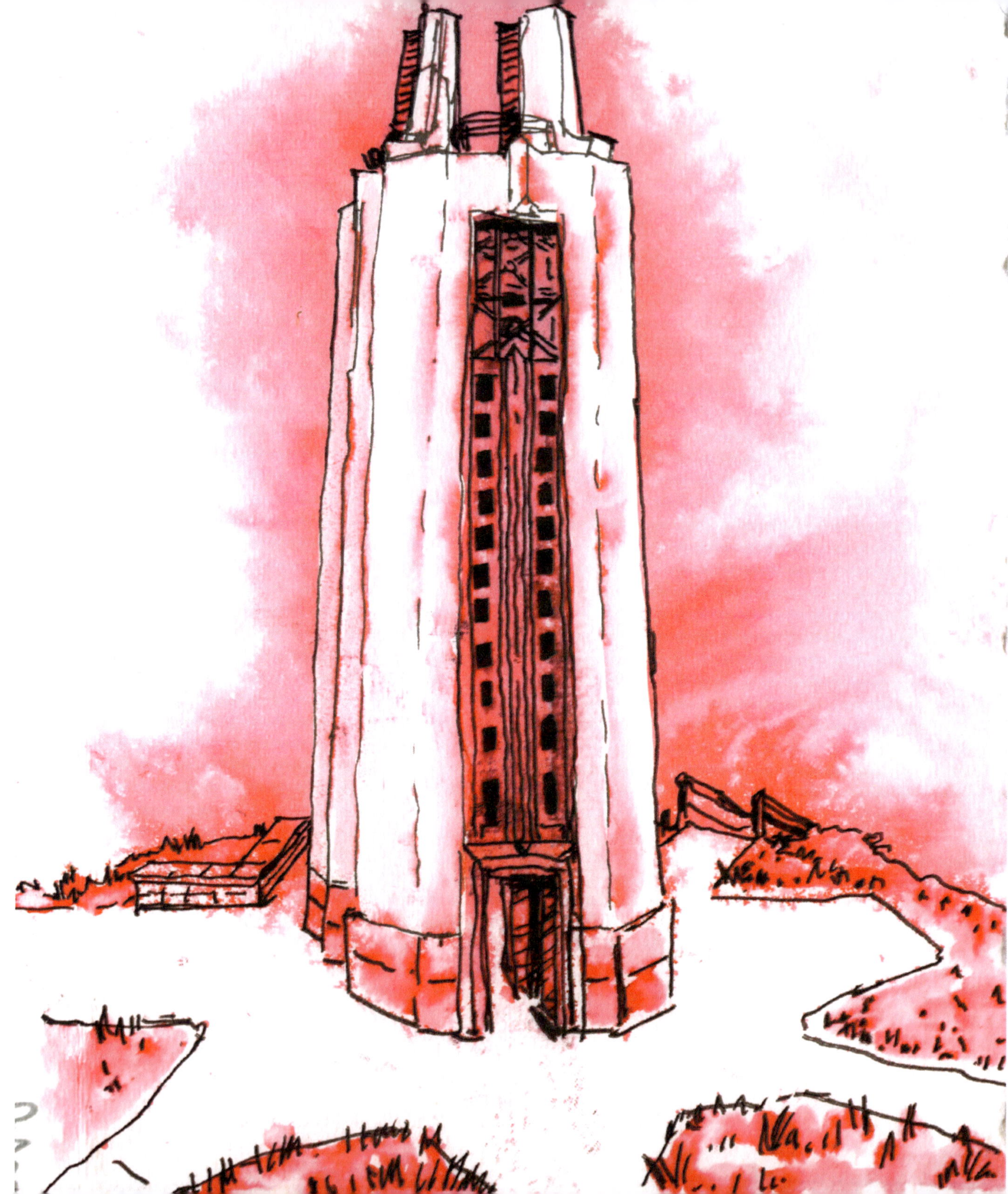

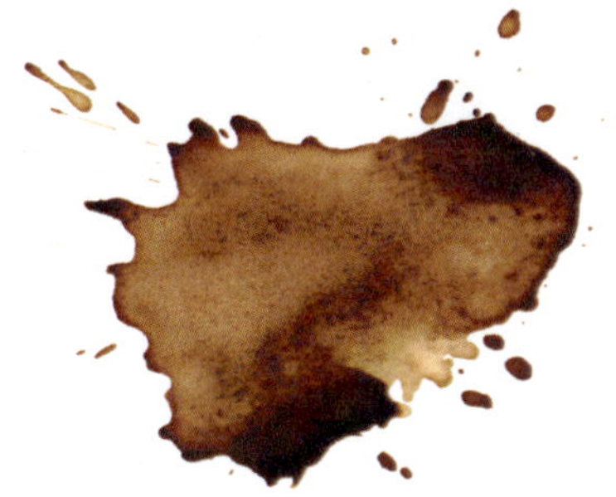

V. Pay Heed

That night the Union burned, red on sweaty faces

the fire that haunted Pete Vinegar one final time

after the frosty silence of the City Commission chamber

after the agony in brick buildings

the shouting and the crying

prison and palace and dormitory and reverberation

of thunder of March over distant mountains.

He who was living is now dead

we who were living are now dying

with a little patience.

Here is no river, but only rock

chalk and no river but the paved highway

the highway stretches faultless across the plains

if there were water, I would not drink

on the highway, one has time to think

sweat is dry, the tires are hot

the water's blood, between the rock

factory lights gape, the mouth cannot spit

here one can neither stand nor lie nor sit

there is not even silence in the factory

but smoke wisping out leaky dreams

there is not even peace in the factory

but sick smogs sneer and snarl

from blackened holes in dirty towers.

                If there were water

and no rock

if there were rock

and also water

a pond

a pool around the rock...

If there were the sound of water only

not seven-year cicadas

and the trains crying

but the sound of water over rock

where the Meadowlark chirps news in the Maple tree.

Drip drop Rock Chalk Rock Chalk Drip Drop

But there is no water.

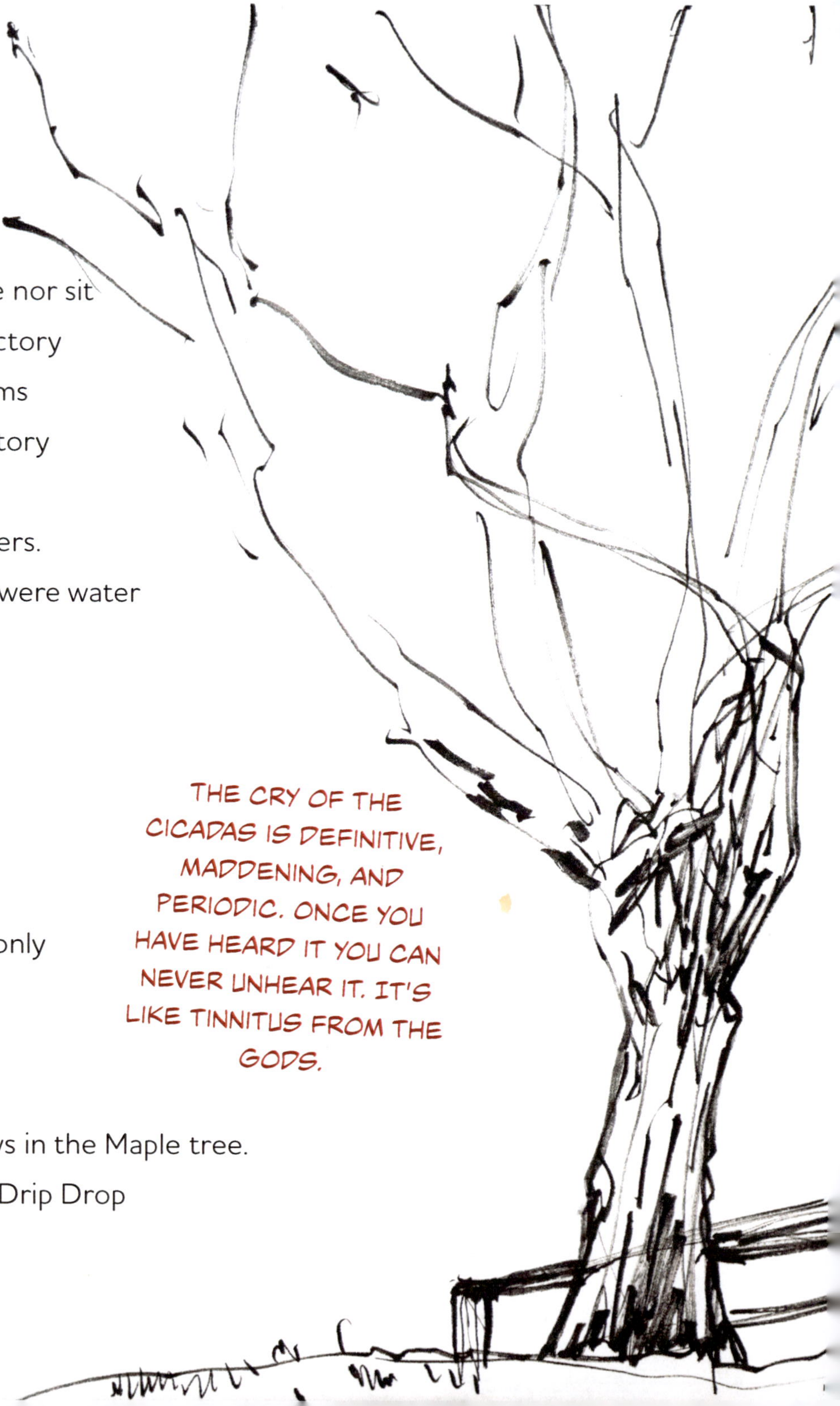

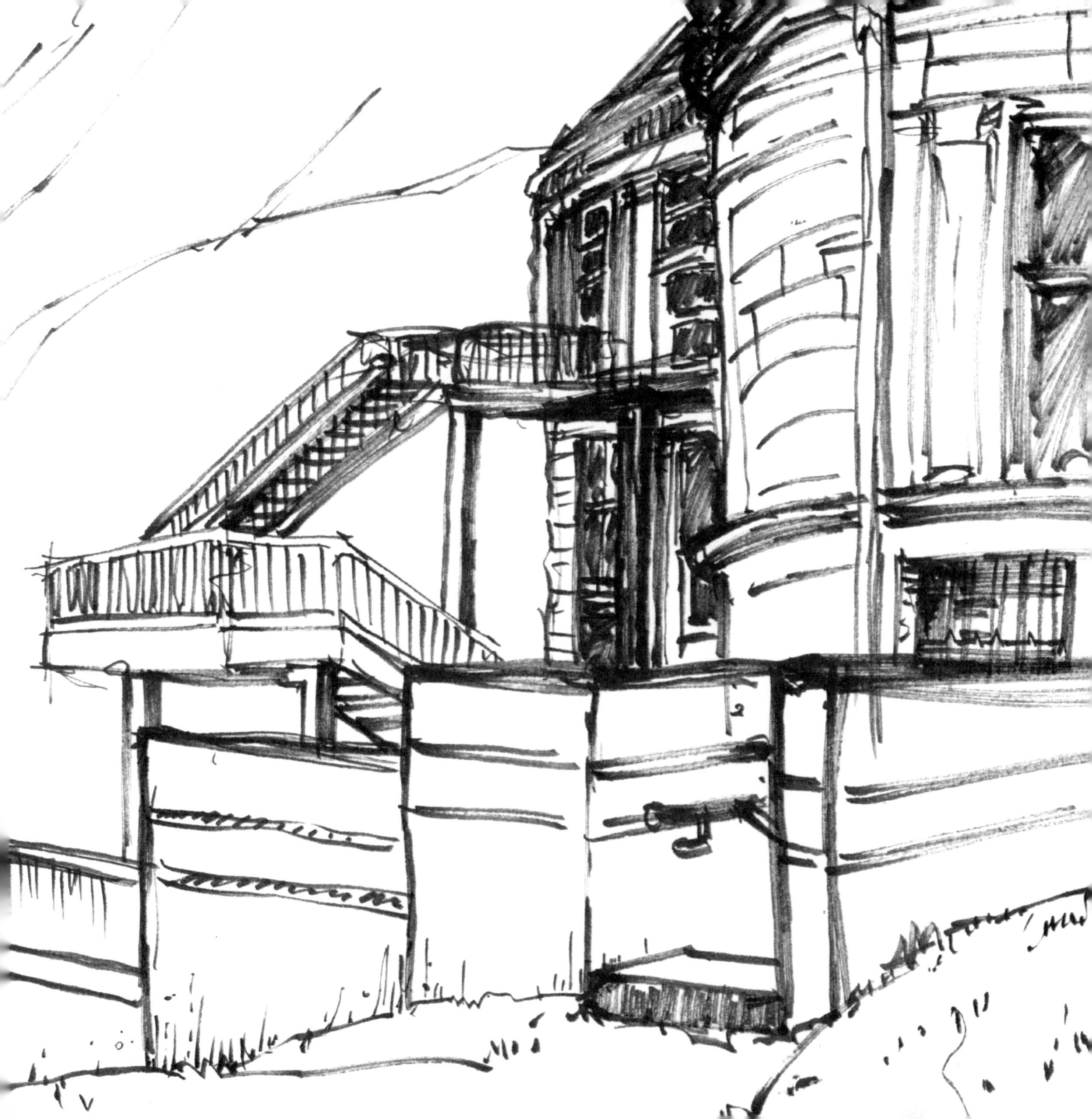

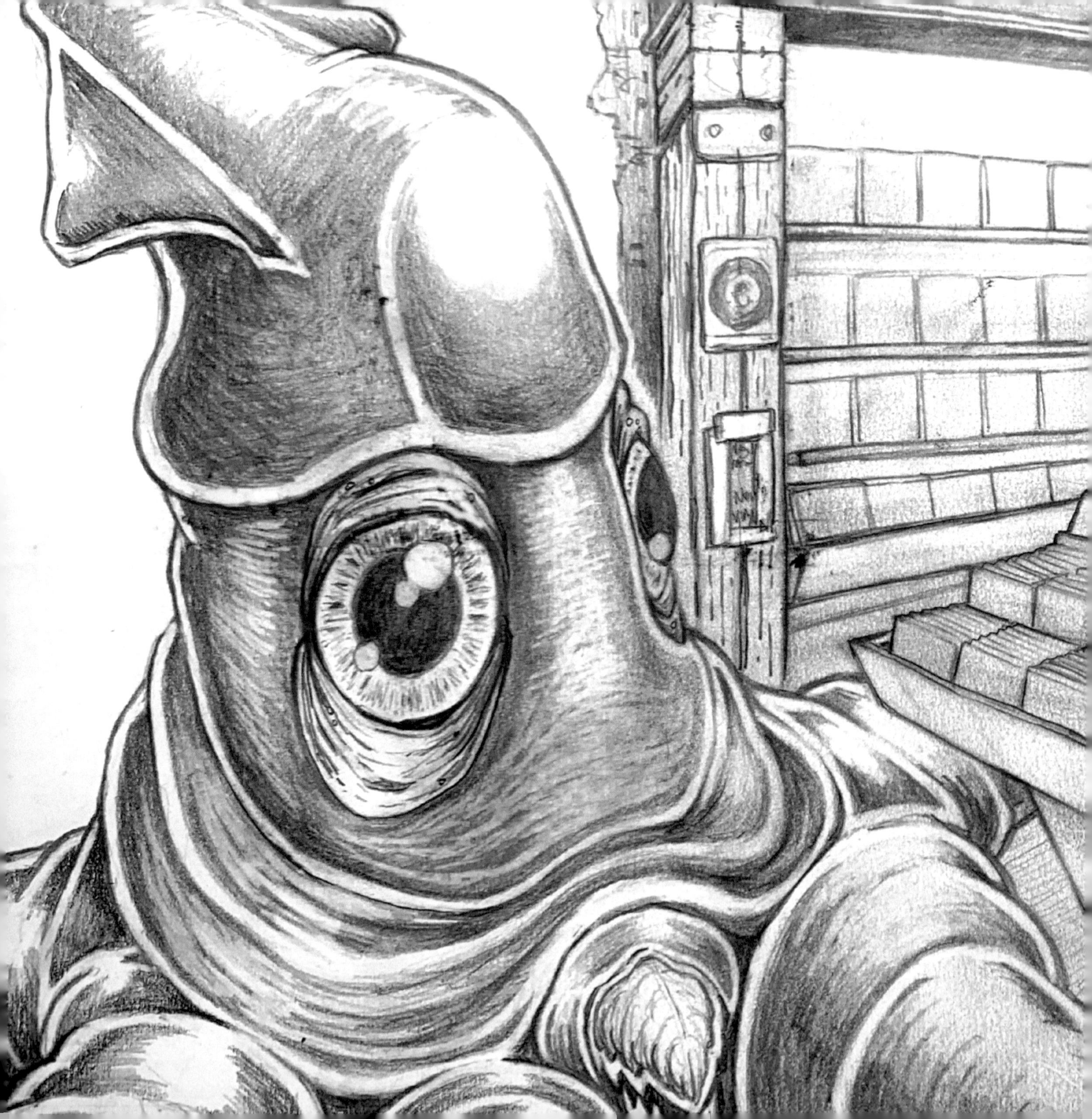

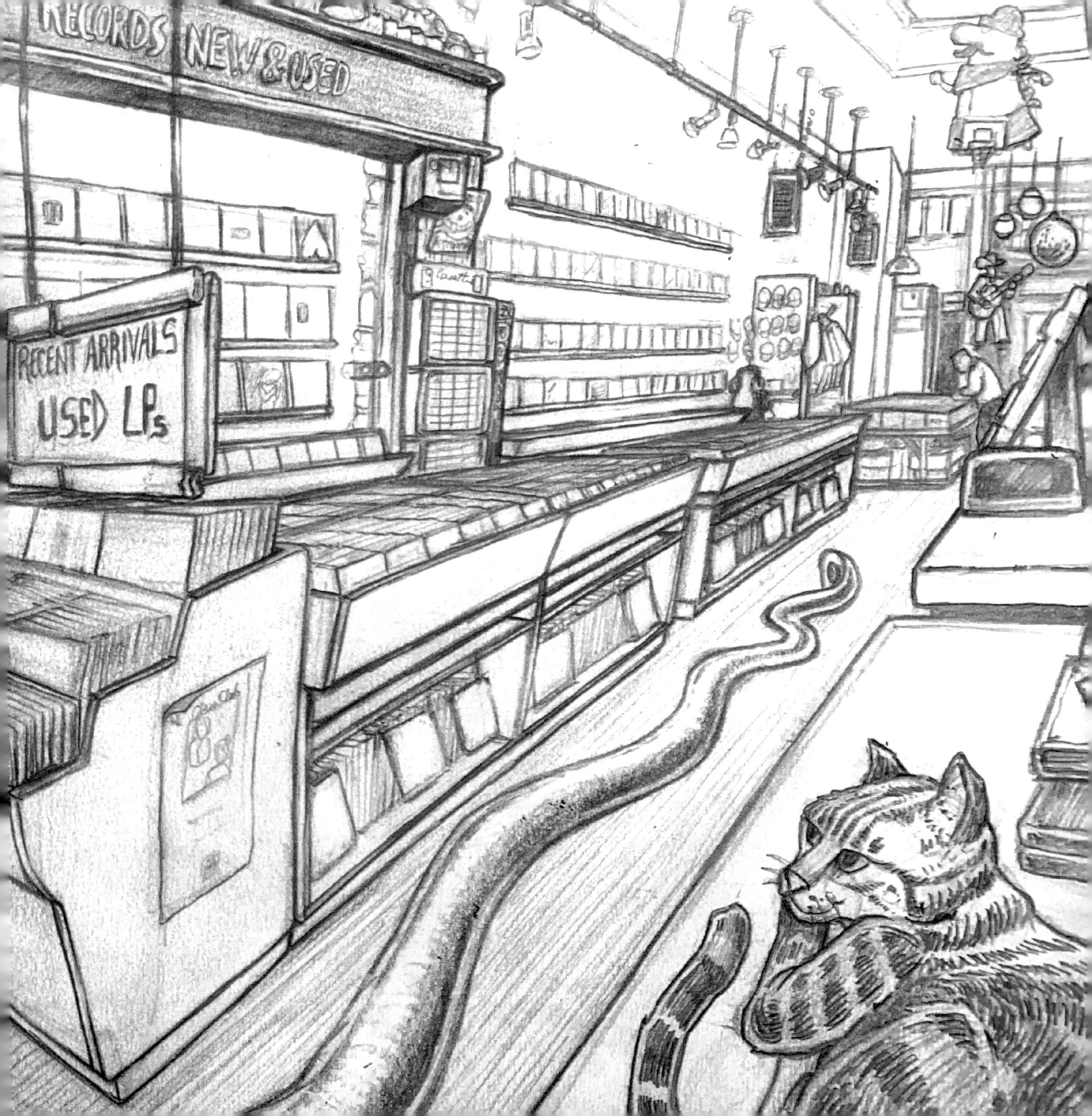

RECORDS NEW & USED
RECENT ARRIVALS
USED LPs

Who is the third who always walks beside you
at last call, there are only you and I together
but when I look ahead toward The Red Lyon
there is always another one walking beside you
head down in a Jayhawk's hoodie,
I do not know how they identify
—but who is on the other side of you?

What is that sound high on the air?
Murmur of maternal lamentation
who are those hoodied hordes swarming
downtown, stumbling over planters
ringed by newly built flats
what is far above the golden valley
cracks and reforms and burst in the violet air
Jayhawk Towers
Reservation Apple Orchards
Naismith Hall Colony Woods.
Unreal.

A Delta Chi drew her long black hair out tight

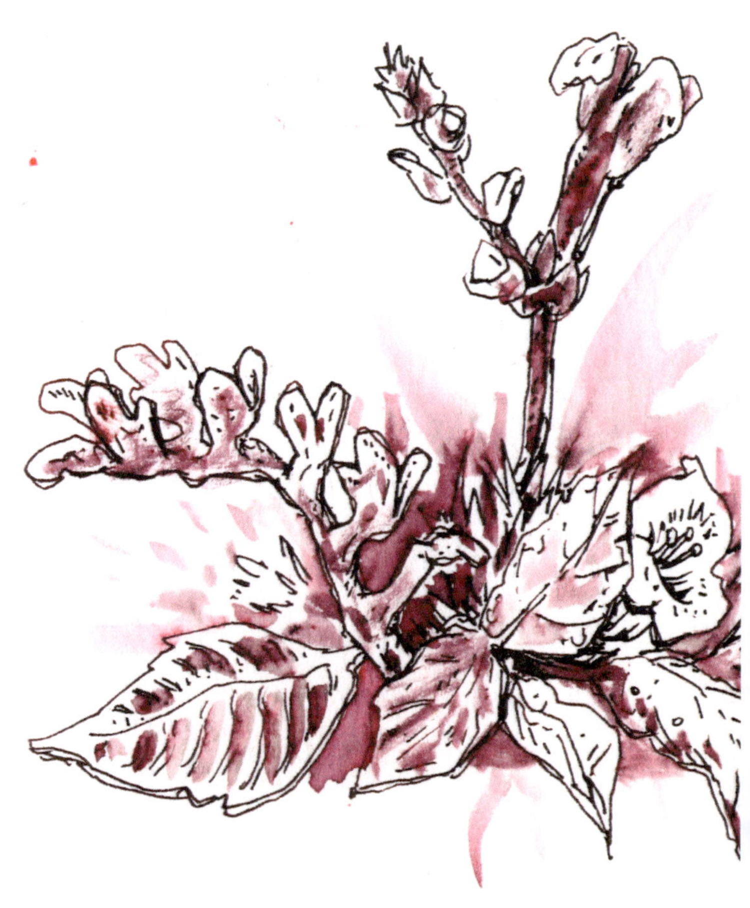

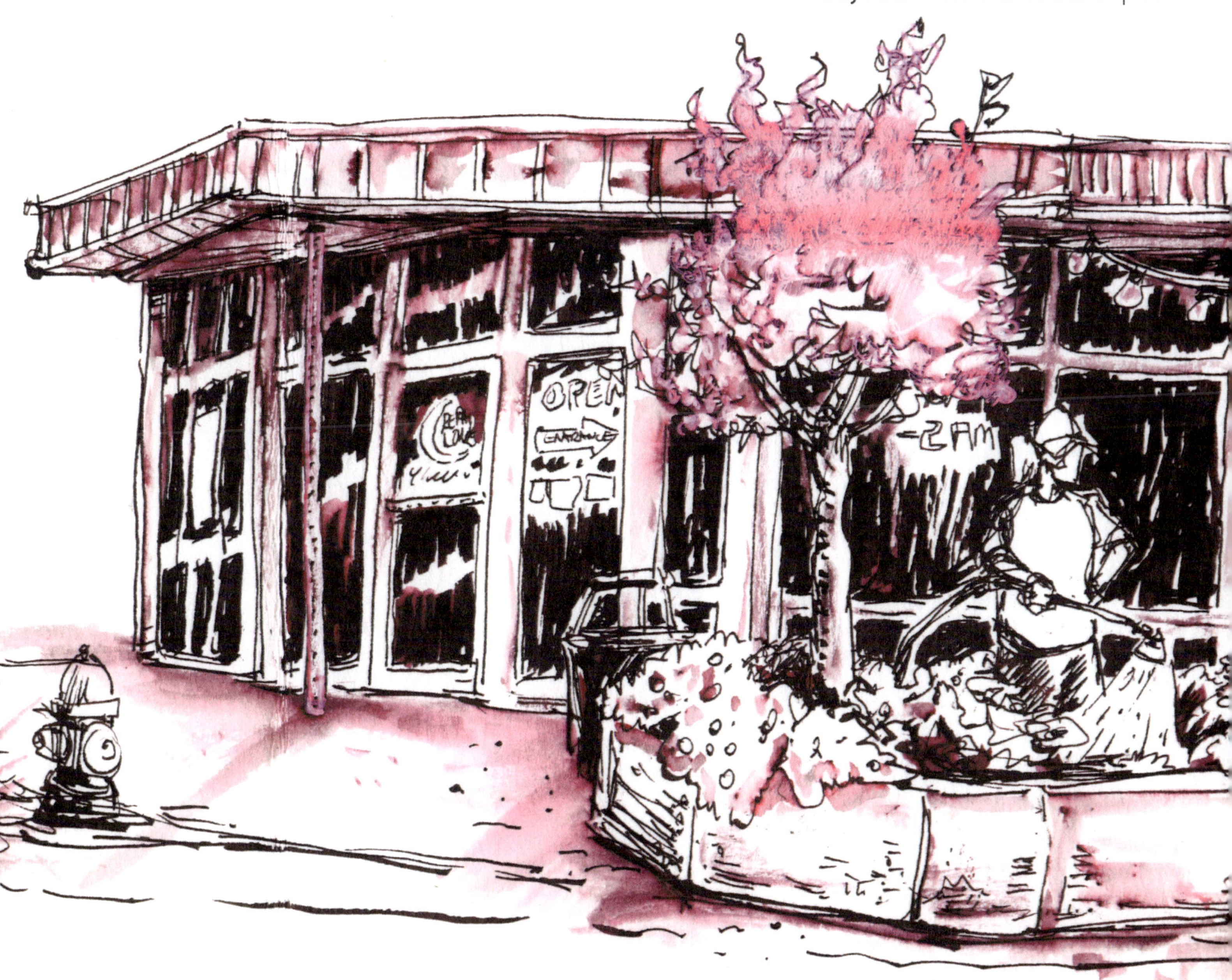

LINDEN, FRUITLESS GINKGO BILOBA, JAPANESE TREE LILAC AND ROSEHILL WHITE ASH ARE ALL USED IN DOWNTOWN PLANTERS.

her Honda's bass is dropped to thunder earth

young birds with baby faces in the violet light

shrieked into Bullwinkles, hell and mirth

and crawled with fake IDs up to the bar

for rounds of drinks which they'd never had before

never sated quickly ordered more

and voices singing out of Logies and The Wheel.

In this decayed bar among the gift shops

Midwest full moon, the beer is pouring

over men in their forties, trees of the bar.

This townie bar, only the wind's home

near no water, the land's Harbour

Lights has few windows and the door swings,

old bones that harm no one.

Only a battered jukebox on the wall

Su Su Sudeo

the crack of pool balls. Breeze as the door opens

bringing rain.

YOUNG BIRDS WITH BABY FACES REFERS TO THE ENDLESS ON-SLAUGHT OF SORORITY GIRLS WHO DESCEND UPON THE TOWN EACH FALL AND LEAVE AGAIN IN THE SPRING, LEAVING NESTS OF UNWANTED HOUSEHOLD ITEMS FOR THE LOCALS TO PICK OVER.

ALLMAN, FROM THE FIRST MOVEMENT, HAS A LIFETIME BAN AT HARBOR LIGHTS. THIS ISN'T RELEVANT TO THE POEM, IT'S JUST FUNNY.

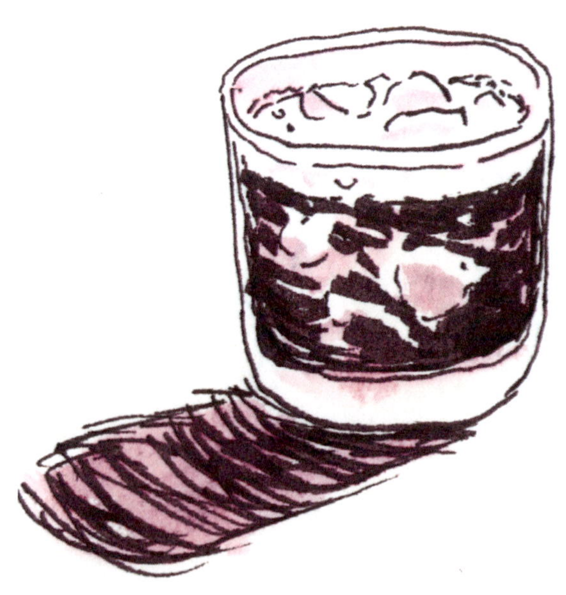

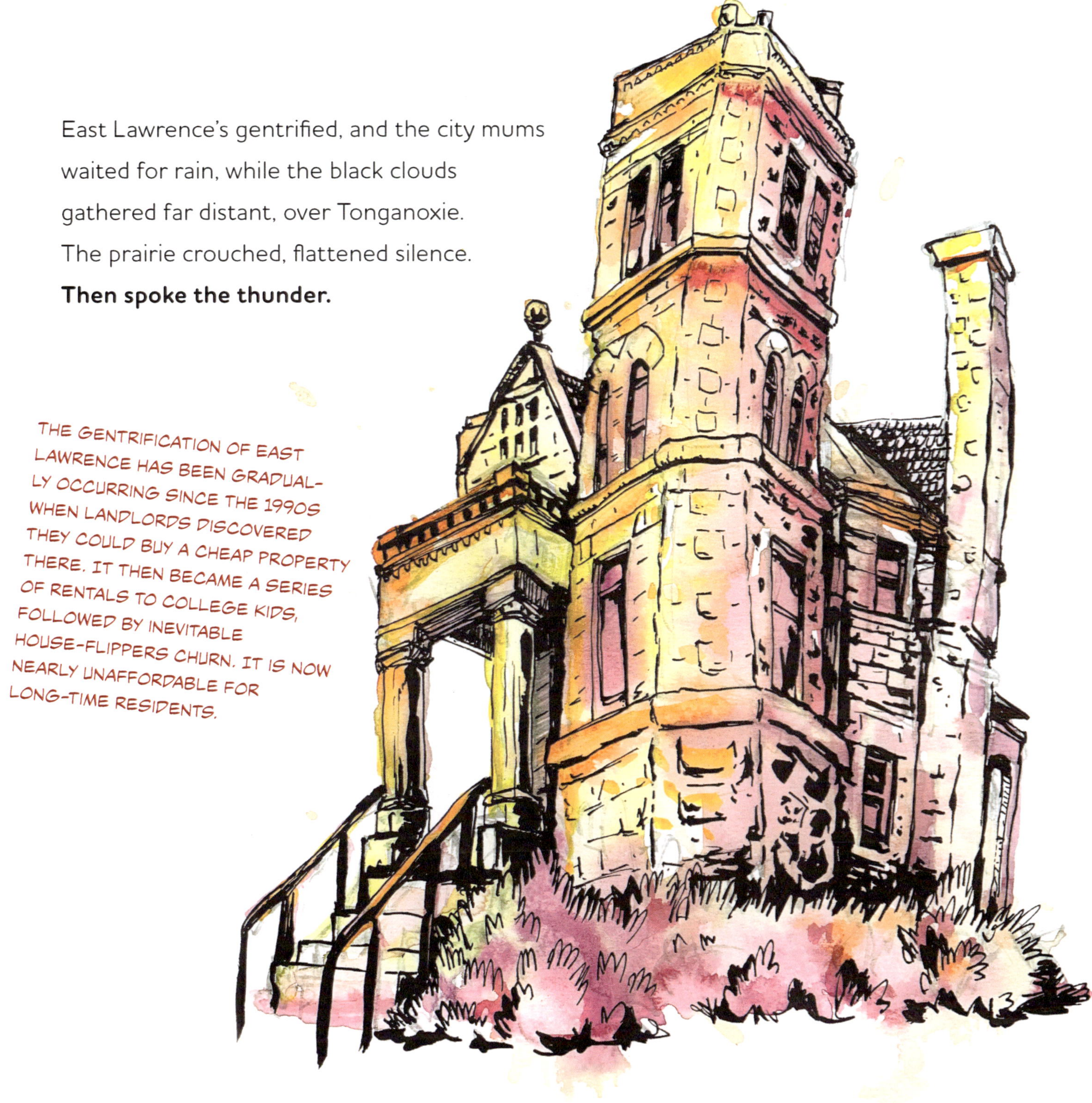

East Lawrence's gentrified, and the city mums
waited for rain, while the black clouds
gathered far distant, over Tonganoxie.
The prairie crouched, flattened silence.
Then spoke the thunder.

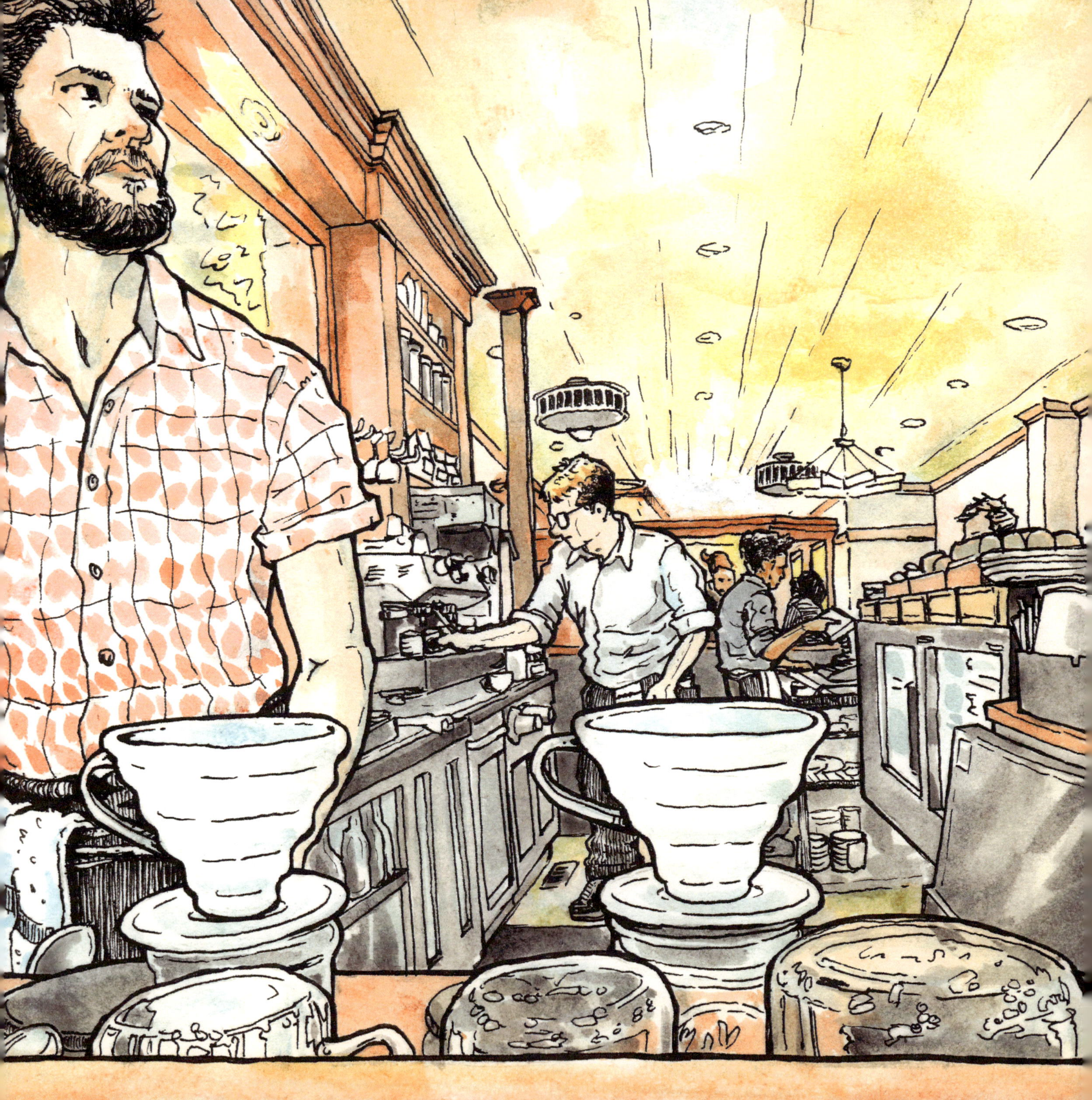

TRY

Lawhorn: What have we given?

The Editor, salsa staining on tie

the humble homespun conservatism

that burning of Unions cannot prevent

by spite, and only spite, we have existed

which is not to be found in obituaries

or in memories muttered in a trivia night

or in tunnels underneath the city

in dorm rooms

TRY

Lawhorn: I have watched The Wheel

churn students into mid-level managers.

We think of The Wheel, each in his fraternity

thinking of The Wheel, each complicit in his fraternity

and then at Nightfall, Bryce says

Put on your Polo, we're going.

TRY

Lawhorn: The city responded

smiling, absorbing the lost

calming the sea, your editorial would have responded

with a joke about chicken wings

with controlling hands.

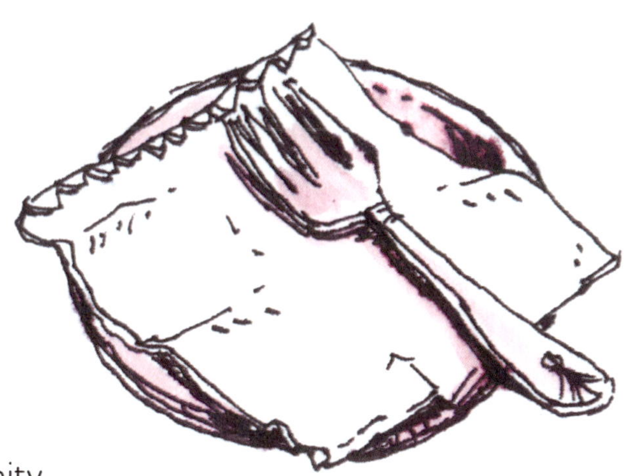

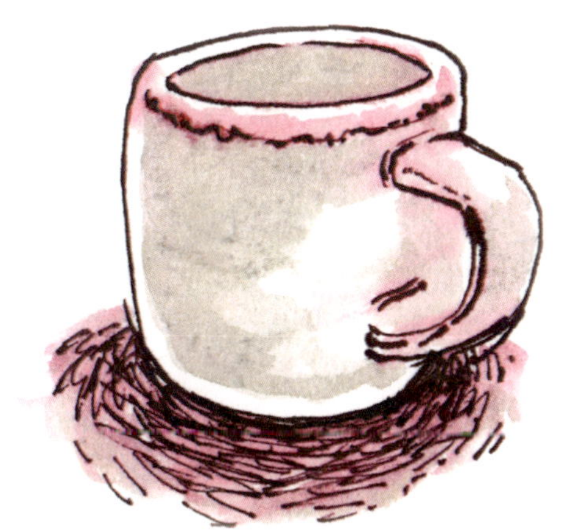

I sat upon the jetty

fishing, the grain elevator rises behind me.

Shall I at least set my lands in order?

Far Above the Gold Valley, Glorious To View

mangia il povero ragazzo a terrebonne

Bibentes bibetis—Chug! Chug!

s'il vous plaît laissez un pourboire au serveur.

These fragments have I shored against my ruins.

Yesterday a night gone thing. A sun-down name.

Try. Try Writing. Try Writing Cursive.

Shout Peace. Shout Peace. Shout Peace.

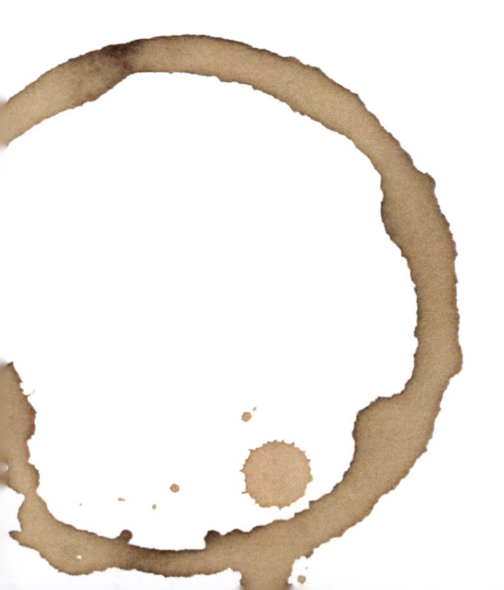

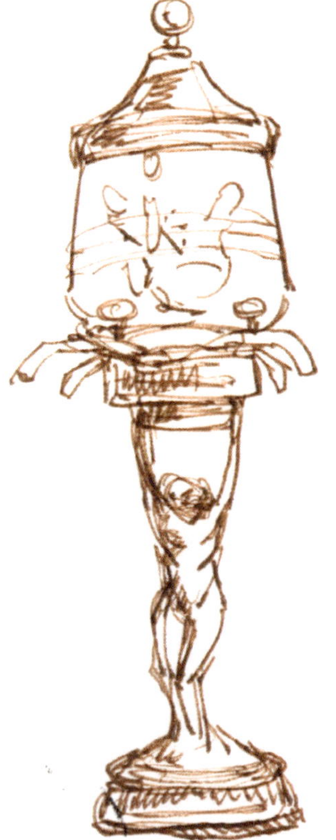

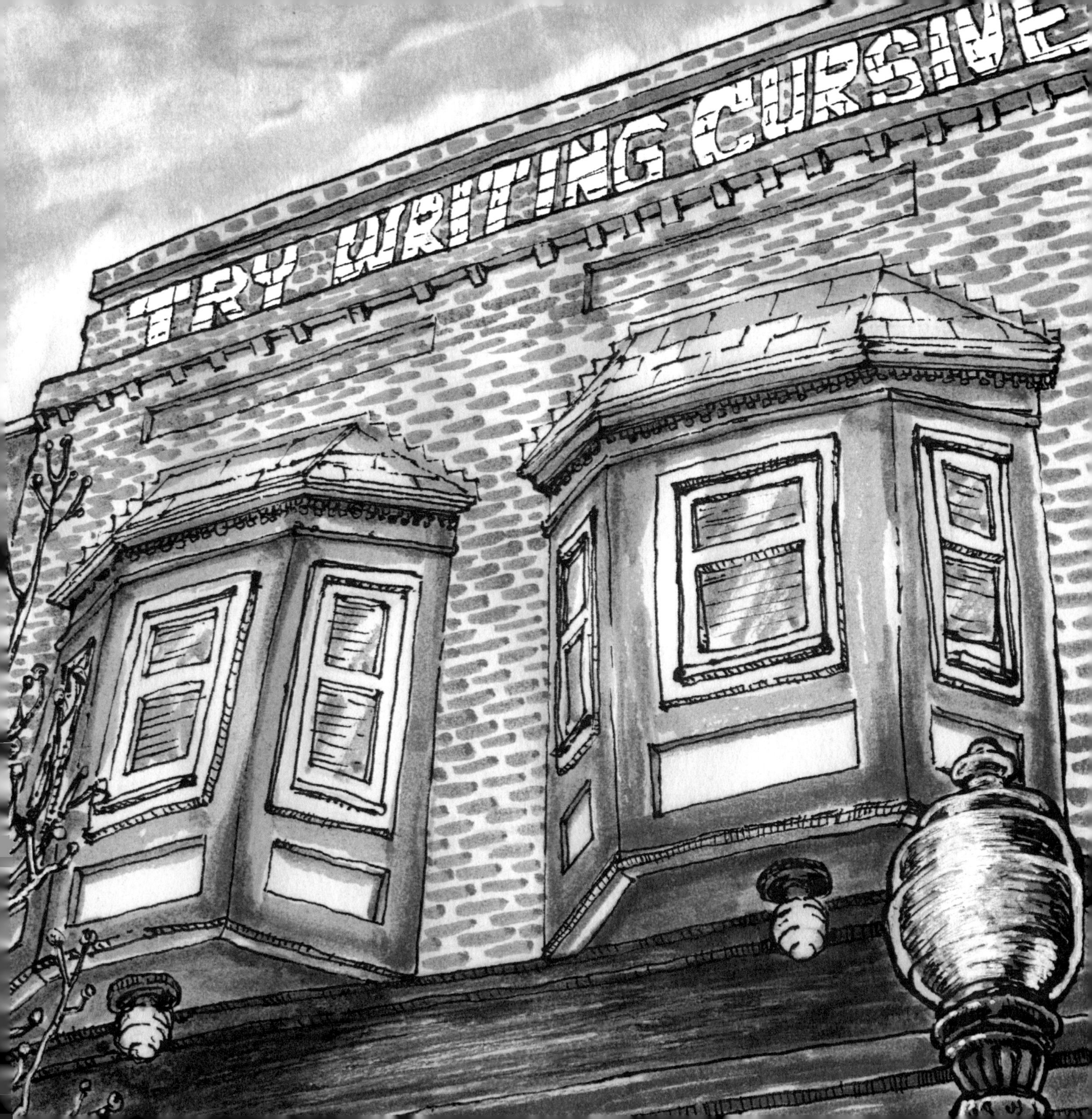

TRY WRITING CURSIVE

About the Author

WILL AVERILL is a writer, actor, puppeteer, expat, and townie. Born at LMH in 1974, Averill grew up on the mean streets of North Lawrence, attending Woodlawn, Broken Arrow, Central, Lawrence High School, and KU (twice). In 1997 Will and co-Artistic Director Jeremy Auman started Card Table Theatre, focusing on new works by Midwest authors, the Victor Continental Comedy Show, and Sh*tty Deal Puppet Theatre Company. In 2003, Averill moved to Norwich, England for eight years, co-founding the theatre company Axis of Evil, performing comedy and puppet shows across the U.K. and Europe, and participating in the Edinburgh Fringe from 2007-2010.

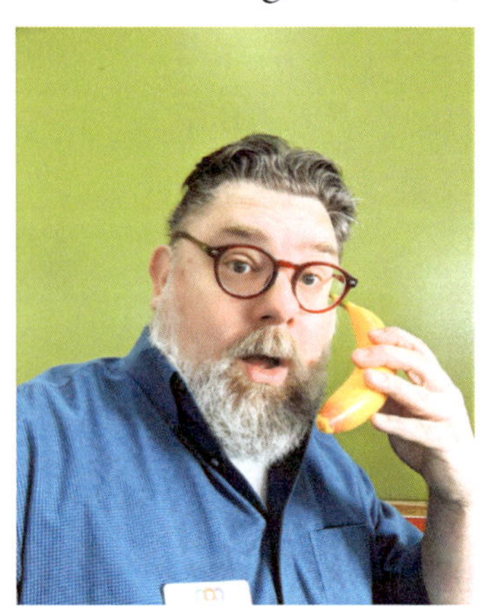

WILL AVERILL

Will's first published work was the short piece "We Reuse Everything" in Central Junior High's literary magazine Inkspots, and it's only gone up from there. His writing includes a series of plays for middle-school students published by Playscripts, Inc., the screenplay "Riding the Pine" (with Ric Averill), the poem and Facebook page "F*ck You, I'm from Kansas," and most recently "King Dale: A Trailer Park Tragedy in Iambic Pentameter (Mostly)." Averill lives in Lawrence with his amazing wife, little old son, and petulant teenage dog, Daisy.

Will really wants to win the Macarthur genius grant, so if you know anyone, hit him up.

About the Artist

KENT SMITH (SMITTY) is a dimension-jumping illustrator, designer, sculptor, teacher, problem-maker, problem-solver, and magic-man sharing grand visions from afar. His work can be found on Star Wars toys, Free State beer labels, custom masks, huge woodblocks prints, giant festival sculptures and tiny trading cards.

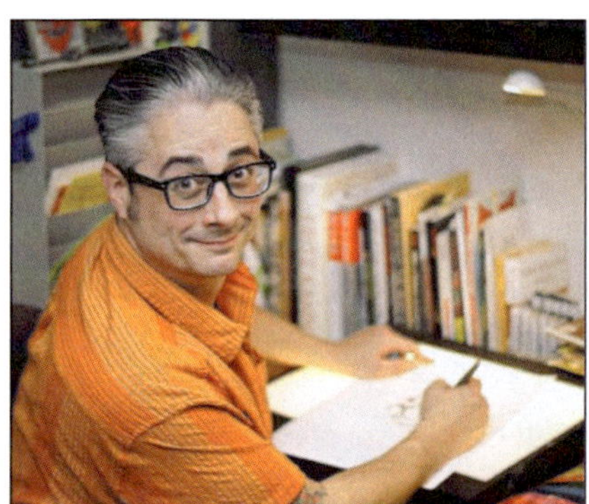

KENT SMITH.
PHOTO BY FALLY AFANI

Smitty uses his crazy brainpowers and a menagerie of media to solve problems and deliver creative, unexpected, solutions that are rich in play and story. Kent also celebrates teaching in the Design Department at the University of Kansas, as well as working with the Lawrence Arts Center, VanGo, Percolator and other fine organizations.

Smitty loves super-heroes, ninjas, monkeys, UFOs, cryptids, robots, ray-guns, and romance. He is always up for creative adventures and hopes you will come visit Smittytown whenever you need a fantastic escape, ridiculous adventure, and fun solutions for your creative needs. You can reach him at: smittytown.com.

We hope you enjoyed Will Averill's and Kent Smith's "DAY AFTER THE WASTELAND." Please order additional print copies from https://anamcara-press.com/